LEARNING GOOD CONSENT

Building Ethical Relationships in a Complicated World

cindy crabb

Learning Good Consent Building Ethical Relationships in a Complicated World

Editing and credited content is © Cindy Crabb, 2010
Contributions are owned by their respective authors
This Edition © Microcosm Publishing, 2010, 2018
Cover by Tom Herpich, ThomasHerpich.com

This is Microcosm #103
ISBN 978-1-62106-667-5
First edition (January 15, 2010) 5,000 copies
Second Edition (June 15, 2018) 5,000 copies

Microcosm Publishing
2752 N Williams Ave.
Portland, OR 97227
www.microcosmpublishing.com
(503) 799-2698

Microcosm Publishing . com

If you bought this on Amazon, that sucks because you could have gotten it cheaper and supported a small, independent publisher at MicrocosmPublishing.com

Microcosm Publishing is Portland's most diversified publishing house and distributor with a focus on the colorful, authentic, and empowering. Our books and zines have put your power in your hands since 1996, equipping readers to make positive changes in their lives and in the world around them. Microcosm emphasizes skill-building, showing hidden histories, and fostering creativity through challenging conventional publishing wisdom with books and bookettes about DIY skills, food, bicycling, gender, self-care, and social justice. What was once a distro and record label was started by Joe Biel in his bedroom and has become among the oldest independent publishing houses in Portland, OR. We are a politically moderate, centrist publisher in a world that has inched to the right for the past 80 years.

Global labor conditions are bad, and our roots in industrial Cleveland in the 70s and 80s made us appreciate the need to treat workers right. Therefore, our books are MADE IN THE USA and printed on post-consumer paper.

Library of Congress Cataloging-in-Publication Data

LEARNING GOOD CONSENT

cindy crabb

intro

learning good consent

I remember when I first heard about verbal consent. I was 22 years old and it was all over the news that Antioch college had passed a sexual assault prevention policy that said you had to ask before each new stage of making out, and that you had to get verbal consent.

In much of the media, it was attacked as some kind of uptight, anti-sex, feminist takeover, but for me, and for a lot of people, it was the beginning of being able to envision and work toward a more healthy sexuality.

Before the Antioch policy, I blamed myself for my inability to say 'no'. Saying 'no' was the only thing I could think of to avoid unwanted sex, and since I couldn't say it, I felt like I just had to go along with whatever. Learning about verbal consent opened up a whole world for me. I started practicing it.

Even though I wished other people would take the initiative and ask <u>me</u> for consent, there was something really empowering and sexy and sweet about constantly asking them 'is this ok?', 'do you want me to do this?'

Sometimes it helped me to realize I wasn't the only one who was scared or unsure. Sometimes checking in with them helped me check in with myself.

For the most part, I didn't know what my own boundries were. and I think learning our boundries is a life long process. We can do some figuring out on our own, but not all of it. and it changes.

and I think it is so very essential that we honor whatever ways we have survived. and that we honor the ways we are surviving now.

Hearing people talk about their own experiences with consent helps me feel less crazy and less alone.

It gives me hope that we will be able to change the world we live in - that we will be able to change what gets taken for granted, and how we see and understand eachother.

Things have already changed. I think it is important to remember this. From the founding of the first rape crisis center, the first feminist women's health center, the first workshop on consent, the forming of groups like Men Can Stop Rape, Sister Song, Philly's Pissed, Generation 5 - these and all the books and zines and conversations and art shows and speakouts and songs and friendships. they are changing things. I can see it. even when there is so much still.

Talking about our experiences with consent, our struggles, our mistakes and how we've learned, these are part of a much larger revolutionary struggle. I feel lucky to have been asked to compile this zine, and am amazed by the bravery of the contributors.

And I am amazed by your bravery too. Yes, you. In a world which asks us not to care too deeply or question too closely, it is brave to be here with this. Learning Good Consent.

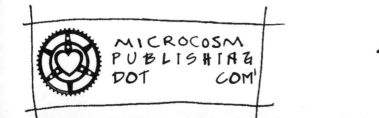

MICROCOSM
PUBLISHING
DOT   COM'

consent questions

from SUPPORT zine

by andrea, cindy + aflea

..Not all of the questions have right or wrong answers. We put them together with the hopes that it would help people to think deeply, and to help open up conversations about consent.
I know it's a long list, but please read and think honestly about these questions, one at a time.

1. How do you define consent?
2. Have you ever talked about consent with your partners(s) or friends?
3. Do you know people, or have you been with people who define consent differently than you do?
4. Have you ever been unsure about whether or not the person you were being sexual with wanted to be doing what you were doing? Did you talk about it? Did you ignore it in hopes that it would change? Did you continue what you were doing because it was pleasurable to you and you didn't want to deal with what the other person was experiencing? Did you continue because you felt it was your duty? How do you feel about the choice you made?
5. Do you think it is the other person's responsibility to say something if they aren't into what you are doing?
6. How might someone express that what is happening is not ok?
7. Do you look only for verbal signs or are there other signs?
8. Do you think it is possible to misinterpret silence for consent?
9. Have you ever asked someone what kinds of signs you should look for if they have a hard time verbalizing when something feels wrong?
10. Do you only ask about these kinds of things if you are in a serious relationship or do you feel able to talk in casual situations too?
11. Do you think talking ruins the mood?
12. Do you think consent can be erotic?
13. Do you think about people's abuse histories?
14. Do you check in as things progress or do you assume the original consent means everything is ok?
15. If you achieve consent once, do you assume it's always ok after that?
16. If someone consents to one thing, do you assume everything else is ok or do you ask before touching in different ways or taking things to more intense levels?
17. Are you resentful of people who need or want to talk about being abused? Why?
18. Are you usually attracted to people who fit the traditional standard of beauty as seen in the united states?
19. Do you pursue friendship with people because you want to be with them, and then give up on the friendship if that person isn't interested in you sexually?
20. Do you pursue someone sexually even after they have said they just want to be friends?
21. Do you assume that if someone is affectionate they are probably sexually interested in you?
22. Do you think about affection, sexuality and boundaries? Do you talk about these issues with people? IF so, do you talk about them only when you want to be sexual with someone or do you talk about them because you think it is important and you genuinely want to know?
23. Are you clear about your own intentions?
24. Have you ever tried to talk someone into doing something they showed hesitancy about?
25. Do you think hesitancy is a form of flirting?

6

26. Are you aware that in some instances it is not?
27. Have you ever thought someone's actions were flirtatious when that wasn't actually the message they wanted to get across?
28. Do you think that if someone is promiscuous that makes it ok to objectify them, or talk about them in ways you normally wouldn't?
29. If someone is promiscuous, do you think it's less important to get consent?
30. Do you think that if someone dresses in a certain way it makes it ok to objectify them?
31. If someone dresses a certain way do you think it means they want your sexual attention or approval?
32. Do you understand that there are many other reasons, that have nothing to do with you, that a person might want to dress or act in a way that you might find sexy?

33. Are you attracted to people with a certain kind of gender presentation?
34. Have you ever objectified someone's gender presentation?
35. Do you assume that each person who fits a certain perceived gender presentation will interact with you in the same way?
36. Do you think sex is a game?
37. Do you ever try to get yourself into situations that give you an excuse for touching someone you think would say "no" if you asked? i.e., dancing, getting really drunk around them, falling asleep next to them.
38. Do you make people feel "unfun" or "unliberated" if they don't want to try certain sexual things?
39. Do you think there are ways you act that might make someone feel that way even if it's not what you're trying to do?
40. Do you ever try and make bargains? i.e. "if you let me _____, I'll do _____ for you"?
41. Have you ever tried asking someone what they're feeling? IF so, did you listen to them and respect them?
42. Have you used jealousy as a means of control?
43. Do you feel like being in a relationship with someone means that they have an obligation to have sex with you?
44. What if they want to abstain from sex for a week? a month? a year?
45. Do you whine or threaten if you're not having the amount of sex or the kind of sex that you want?
46. Do you think it's ok to initiate something sexual with someone who's sleeping?
47. What if the person is your partner?
48. Do you think it's important to talk with them about it when they're awake first?
49. Do you ever look at how you interact with people or how to treat people, positive or negative, and where that comes from/ where you learned it?
50. Do you behave differently when you've been drinking?
51. What are positive aspects of drinking for you? What are negative aspects?
52. Have you been sexual with people when you were drunk or when they were drunk? Have you ever felt uncomfortable or embarrassed about it the next day? Has the person you were with ever acted weird to you afterward?
53. Do you seek consent the same way when you are drunk as when you're sober?
54. Do you think it is important to talk the next day with the person you've been sexual with if there has been drinking involved? If not, is it because it's uncomfortable or because you think something might have happened that shouldn't have? Or is it because you think that's just the way things go?
55. Do you think people need to take things more lightly?
56. Do you think these questions are repressive and people who look critically at their sexual histories and their current behavior are uptight and should be more "liberated"?

57. Do you think liberation might be different for different people?
58. Do you find yourself repeating binary gender behaviors, even within queer relationships and friendships? How might you doing this make others feel?
59. Do you view sexuality and gender presentation as part of a whole person, or do you consider those to be exclusively sexual aspects of people?
60. If someone is dressed in drag, do you take it as an invitation to make sexual comments?
61. Do you fetishize people because of their gender presentation?
62. Do you think only men abuse?
63. Do you think that in a relationship between people of the same gender, only the one who is more "manly" abuses?

64. How do you react if someone becomes uncomfortable with what you're doing, or if they don't want to do something? Do you get defensive? Do you feel guilty? Does the other person end up having to take care of you and reassure you? or are you able to step back and listen and hear them and support them and take responsibility for your actions?
65. Do you tell your side of the story and try and change the way they experienced the situation?
66. Do you do things to show your partner that you're listening and that you're interested in their ideas about consent or their ideas about what you did?
67. Do you ever talk about sex and consent when you're not in bed?
68. Have you ever raped or sexually abused or sexually manipulated someone? Are you able to think about your behavior? Have you made changes? What kinds of changes?

69. Are you uncomfortable with your body or your sexuality?
70. Have you been sexually abused?
71. Has your own uncomfortable ness or your own abuse history caused you to act in abusive ways? If so, have you ever been able to talk to anyone about it? Do you think talking about it is or could be helpful?
72. Do you avoid talking about consent or abuse because you aren't ready to or don't want to talk about your own sexual abuse?
73. Do you ever feel obligated to have sex?
74. Do you ever feel obligated to initiate sex?
75. What if days, months, or years later. someone tells you they were uncomfortable with what you did? Do you grill them?
76. Do you initiate conversations about safe sex and birth control (if applicable)?
77. Do you think that saying something as vague as "I've been tested recently" is enough?
78. Do you take your partners concerns about safe sex and/or birth control seriously?
79. Do you think that if one person wants to have safe sex and the other person doesn't really care, it is the responsibility of the person who has concerns to provide safe sex supplies?
80. Do you think if a person has a body that can get pregnant, and they don't want to, it is up to them to provide birth control?
81. Do you complain or refuse safe sex or the type of birth control your partner want to use because it reduces your pleasure?
82. Do you try and manipulate your partner about these issues?
83. Do you think there is ongoing work that we can do to end sexual violence in our communities?

queers, kissing and accountability

By Shannon Perez-Darby

I have this muscle memory of distrust. My first instinct is to pull away; it's to push you away. I want to distrust you,

I want you to push a little further because that's familiar because, "the devil you know is better than the devil you don't..." or however that goes. I want to learn how to do it differently. I want to teach my body another way of being. For me all of this learning, sex, abuse, power, crossed boundaries, panic attacks and anxiety, it all lives inside my body. My body reacts from its memory, from the ways it's learned to be.

So how do I do it differently? I work at a domestic violence organization and my job is essentially to talk about relationships. My job is healing and triggering all at once. When I think back to crossed boundaries, to consent, to the moments I've been asked about what I want, how I want to be touched and how I don't want to be touched my answer is silence more often than not.

You can ask for consent, be willing to hear yes and no, you can be engaged and present but if I'm too hurt to sit with you, to sit in my body with my responses and feelings then where does that leave me? When I think about accountability I think about all the ways I've learned to go along with it, to make things easy and to not make waves. There are so many moments when it's easier to say nothing, to not have to speak up or define my edges for you. I get to hide in the blurriness. It feels less scary to say nothing and pickup the pieces inside of myself than say no and have to discover where I start and you stop. I get lost in the messy places between us and that's not love and that's not accountability. For me accountability is showing up with my whole self, it's being present and brave enough to actually be somewhere with someone instead of hiding in my own insecurities, fear and internalized shit. I want to do better than hiding. I know I can do better than sort of showing up.

As someone who mostly has sex with other folks socialized as girls, communication around consent in my life and communities is different than how I was taught growing up. For me, being a homo has meant a shift in how I understand my role when it comes to sex. When I was younger I was less of an active participant in the sex I was having and more of a referee. I never said "touch me here" or "I like it like this" but instead let whatever boy I was kissing do whatever he thought was sexy and my job was to make sure it never went too far over the (my) line. I was a gatekeeper always guarding whatever felt like the most vulnerable part of myself. Generally, by the time I was willing to use my voice we were several steps ahead of where I actually wanted to be. I would wait until the scales tipped, until whatever sexy place we were going was scarier than saying "stop."

When I think about these interactions I'm filled with all of these contradictory things. I would call some of these experiences coercive and I struggle with the language all of the time. These are the moments when accountability feels muddled. I believe the guys I was having sexual interactions with were doing the best they could. I believe that they wanted to have mutually pleasurable sex and that they wished the best for me. For me it doesn't feel like an answer to say that they were all jerks or "evil perpetrators" that I then get to demonize. I believe that the men I was being sexy with had some pretty shitty skills and fucked up expectations and they didn't know how to do it better, which doesn't mean that they shouldn't be accountable for their actions but they also shouldn't be demonized for them either. When we make people evil it dehumanizes everyone.

I'm not sure how much energy it makes sense to put into this idea because then again I'm centering on them on their experiences and not mine. But I do want to push my communities to look at community accountability models. I'm not sure we have all of the skills to be enacting sustainable community accountability models at this exact moment but I think we can be talking more about sexual assault within our own radical communities and how we extend the values of community, social justice and anti-oppression into our conversations around consent and accountability in our sexual interactions.

Saying that I don't want to demonize the people who have been sexually coercive has become easier to talk about because for the most part these interactions are far away, they're in the past and none of these guys are in my life anymore. We were working off of this hetero script that says that guys are the drivers, they will go as far as they can with a girl and it's the girls job to be the breaks, always guarding against men who will try to get as much as they can from her sexually unless we put a stop to it. This script is a setup for everyone. It's a setup for the folks doing masculinity because there is no space to have a full range of emotions, to not want to have sex, or to feel anything other than sex crazed, always looking for and wanting sex. It's a setup for women because whatever happens is our fault. Either we don't say anything and silence is consent or we say speak up and we are trouble makers or prudes.

I don't want to setup a false dichotomy that straight men are inherently coercive and queers are radical and thus having only equitable (sexual) relationships because that's not true, and that idea is getting in the way of creating community accountability models. Homos protect the fucked up things we do to each other and it's scary to talk about because what if that proves all of the fucked up things homophobic society says about us? What if we can't have equable relationships? What if we are pedophiles? What if we really can't have healthy relationships? Not talking about it is not keeping us safe, it's keeping us isolated and it's making sure that we perpetuate the same shitty coercive dynamics that we have learned. It means that when coercion and sexual assault happens in our queer communities we don't talk about it, we internalize our oppression and we stay hidden.

I want more models for the relationships and kinds of sex I want to be having in my life. Sometimes the queers in my life pretend that we're more radical than coercion and abuse, that this stuff doesn't affect us, and that it doesn't seep into our sex lives and relationships. Pretending that I'm more "down" than you, that I'm more radical and liberated reinforces the same stuff I'm trying to unlearn. It makes us feel like we are not enough. I'm tired of us all feeling like we're not ok. What would it look like to believe that we could do it another way, that we could do it a million other ways? What would our sexual interactions look like if we believed that we were ok, if we were allowed to be our whole selves, if we saw ourselves as whole? What would it look like to be able to sit with our fears and to engage in a process of accountability with each other? What if we were able to show up in a centered, solid, whole, and graceful way? What would accountability look like? What would we need to even imagine this?

The scariest thing I can think to say to someone that I'm having sex with is that I don't want to have sex. What does my accountability process look like around this? What does consent look like when I'm not even sure I could tell you no? I don't think this is the most loving way I can show up. When our scripts shifts and I'm the one touching you, I'm initiating sex and I'm no longer the brakes but actively engaged then what does consent look like? All of a sudden my responsibility shifts. I've trained myself to go with the flow and now I have a more equitable role in asking how you like to be touched, how you don't want to be touched, what's too light and what's not hard enough and not just once but all the time, it's a constant process of engagement. When I look at this power shift it's a re-envisioning of the sex I had when I was younger. I can feel the complexity and layers to the ways that we learn how to treat each other. You can have someone's best intentions in mind and that doesn't mean that you won't fuck up. That's the scariest thing, sometimes when it comes to crossing people boundaries it doesn't matter where your heart is. That is to say that we can be trying our best and still cross each other boundaries.

That's not to say that intention isn't important. Intention sometimes makes the difference in my healing process but mostly my experience has been that I can't really know what's happening for other folks. We have a lot invested in people that perpetrate sexual assault as evil villains and people that are surviving sexual assault as perfect angels. This narrative hurts us all because it's not about good or evil but about power. Often we get power without asking for it and giving power away can feel counter intuitive because it's something we're not taught to do and have almost no models for. Mostly people who have power and privilege don't necessarily feel like they do. So if coercion is generally about power and most people that have power don't feel like they do then where does that leave us when we're trying to negotiate sex; when we're talking about consent, how to say yes and how to say no? How do we know when we have the power, how do we figure out how to shift power dynamics and what do we do when we use our power (intentionally or not) in fucked up ways? How do we hear and respond when someone says they're not feeling heard or that they feel like their lines have been crossed? How do we honor what an amazing thing it is that someone is even able to say that at all?

Accountability is a process and part of that process is screwing up. That's so scary and so real because when the stakes are this high screwing up doesn't really feel like an option. But what if instead we see accountability as a process we get to engage with when we fuck up, that fucking up is going to happen and instead of denial and hiding, instead of saying that we didn't know any better (whether that's true or not) we apologize, figure out what was going on for us, what places inside of us our actions are centered in and then figure out what we're going to do about it. Because screwing up is a part of the deal but that doesn't mean we get to fuck up in the same way over and over again. We engage so we don't keep fucking up in the exact same ways. I want to fuck up in totally new ways.

In order to do this we have to be coming from a place where we assume that people are trying their hardest and where people really are trying they're hardest. Because the reality is that people do really shitty things to each other all of the time and frankly I don't know how to make sense of that. As a survivor of abuse, as a domestic violence advocate, as a friend and a person in community with other people I've seen and heard some of the really shitty awful things that people do to each other. Folks call us all of the time with really heavy hard stories and those are true and real and everyone makes sense of their experiences and finds healing in ways that are real for them. I feel like I can't say it too much, healing is a process.

Accountability is not taking all of the responsibility and apologizing forever. We all know the script; someone screws up and when they're called on it their response is, "It's all my fault, how could I do this, I am a terrible person, how could you even like me?" In this script the person who didn't necessarily mess up ends up comforting the person who is trying to be accountable. It's a way of looking like we're being accountability without actually having to apologize and look at our actions. Sometimes this seems almost like accountability but really it's a mask that keeps us from sitting with ourselves and getting real about what's going on with us. I choose to believe that the people in my life are doing the best they can. That doesn't mean that they get to treat me badly or do shitty things. Holding this complexity has often been very painful for me, jumping from unearned trust in people who keep crossing my boundaries and not respecting me to martyrdom, so that someone fucks up I keep throwing myself into the fire saying, "they're doing the best they can". I believe there can be a place in between, a place where I can be real with myself and present for the constant engagement it takes to be good to the people in my life and demand respect and kindness.

ASK

here are some ways to ask in the
heat of the moment. but don't forget
talking about it when you're not half
naked is always better

may i_____?
    touch_____?
    kiss _____?
    put my_____ _____?
Are you into this?
How are you feeling?
What would you like me to do?
I think it;s hot when my partner
does _____ to me.
What do you like?
Would you like it if i _____?
Where do you see this going?
What should I look for if you
    start to shut down?

DEFINE

how do you define consent?
  write it down
      and keep it in your pocket

HOMEWORK

write a list of your goals for
future sex and then write how
to achieve them.
keep it in your pocket

write a list of current boundaries
keep it in your pocket

When I was 18, I was raped by my best friend since Kindergarten. We were both drunk and snuggling, and, while I was passed out in his bed, he 'lost' his virginity to me. The next morning, I woke up naked, thinking I had cheated on my boyfriend, and ran across campus to my dorm. At that time, I didn't understand what consent and rape really looked like in everyday life; I didn't tell anyone for 3 years. However, he did; to all our mutual friends. I spent the next 3 years living with the knowledge that all our friends thought I had cheated on my boyfriend. Hell, I thought I had cheated on my boyfriend.

Thinking I was a slut, a bad woman, I broke up with my boyfriend, and spent nights fucking around with boys who didn't give two shits about me; asking things like "do you want me to fuck you again," as I tried to drunkenly fall asleep in their bed; holding up my limp, intoxicated body as they rammed themselves inside of me, ignoring my lack of participation. I didn't have the capacity to understand what consensual sex could look like anymore, until years later, after I declared myself a women's studies major, and began actively thinking of myself as an anarchist, when I realized what had happened to me. I had words for what happened, and they didn't sound anything like "cheating." I was raped, sexually assaulted, violated.

I began talking about it to everyone; I told a class of two hundred college students; I told my next boyfriend (who was once best friends with the first boy who had raped me, and was actually my first real boyfriend years before). We learned how to have sex that pushed my boundaries, engaging in bondage play and becoming more comfortable asking for sex when we wanted it.

But I also learned that by not dealing with my own shit, I was engaging in coercive behavior with him. When he wasn't in the mood, I would pout until he gave in. I couldn't deal with being rejected; it made me feel as though I was a whore with a sex drive that wouldn't quit, or like a needy, pushy, overbearing female. It made me feel terrible about myself.

It made me feel terrible about myself. But what felt worse was that he refused to tell me when I was pushing him too far, or to get angry with me. I began to realize that I was scaring my own partner so much, and was too absorbed by my own trauma, that he didn't feel safe telling me when I was hurting him. Because he didn't want me to feel like the kind of person who would willingly coerce their partner, or couldn't see their own bad behavior. He wanted to protect me from myself, while I dealt with the trauma of being raped. I love him for it still, but I do wish that we could have found some way to deal with my coercive behavior too; I'm still learning how to do this. I need to be called out on my shit. But we just couldn't seem to do that with one another; we broke up after three years together.

Now, I'm with someone who will tell me when I'm pressuring him; if I slap him during sex and it doesn't feel right, we stop and talk about it. We're trying our best to make a non monogamous relationship work, dealing with our jealousy and abandonment issues, while still allowing each other the space we need to do what we want, have sex with who we want, and ultimately not drive each other so crazy that we don't want to be together anymore. Being with this partner is amazing in other ways for me though, in that I'm learning how to give up control in sex, and engage in sex that allows me to slip into roles where i can (safely) be controlled. It's amazing to think about myself becoming capable of expanding what sex can be for myself, and learning to overcome so many of the feelings that stemmed from my rape, shit i couldn't put together while i was with my last 2 partners. It's also really amazing (and terrifying) to have someone around to point out when I'm engaging in coercive or manipulative behavior. We continue to have discussions around the understanding that "perpetrator" and "survivor" are not mutually exclusive terms. And while it's hard to hear someone i love tell me that I'm making him feel unsafe and being manipulative, I'm also really grateful that there is someone willing to stick with me while i deal with this shit.

What Is Saftey?
excerpt from Survivors Guide to Sex by Staci Haines

Most people think of safety as a "feeling" of being safe. While this is one way to judge safety, it is not always reliable. You can be in a very safe situation and feel unsafe because you are dealing with an aspect of your abuse. Or, because you are a trauma survivor, you may be in an unsafe situation and feel just fine. While feeling safe is important, it does not necessarily give you reliable ground on which to determine if you are safe, or safe enough to proceed.

WHAT TELLS YOU THAT YOU ARE SAFE?

1   How do you feel in your body?

2   Is your physical environment safe and free of violence and abuse? (No one is hitting, kicking, punching, or pushing you. No one is calling you names or threatening you or anyone you care about.)

3   Does your partner, lover, or friend consider your needs, wants, and desires as important and relevant as his or her own?

4   Can your partner, lover, or friend really meet your need? Does he or she have the know-how, the tools, and the good intention?

5   Do you have the power in this situation to act upon your own behalf? To take care of yourself fully?

6   Are you making your own choices? Not being pressured, pushed, or manipulated?

Asking yourself these questions gives you a way to assess whether or not you are safe—even when you do not necessarily feel safe.

Write about the following. Then, have a conversation with a friend or therapist about what you wrote.

1.   Take a sexual self-inventory. What have you experienced sexually up to now? What did you like? What did you not like? What do you know about your sexuality? What would you like to learn?

2.   Take a piece of paper and make three columns, titled "yes," "maybe," and "no." In the "yes" column, list all the sexual activities that you enjoy or think you would enjoy. In the "maybe" column, list all the sexual activities that you enjoy under certain circumstances or that you might be willing to try. In the "no" column, list all the sexual activities that you do not enjoy and do not want to explore. Include both masturbation and partner sex. Now, look at your lists. Which column most closely resembles your current sex life?

3.   Imagine an activity that is physically pleasurable to you, enlivening to your senses. It could be walking on warm sand, feeling the breeze against your face, touching your partner, having oral sex. Imagine yourself in that scene now. What kinds of sensations are you feeling while you experience this specific pleasure? Where in your body do you feel them? How much pleasure or desire can you take in?

4.   What sexual activity or fantasy would you like to try out? Be explicit. What's stopping you?

13.

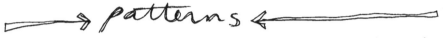

patterns

I was raised to believe that guys wanted sex all the time, and that if they didn't get off when they were turned on then they'd get blue-balls which was totally painful and terrible. I was raised to believe that it was my job to do what was needed. I was abused when I was young, and then dated much older guys, but when I was 18 I was in a relationship with someone my age. One time when he was out of town, I read his journal. (which, needless to say, was a really terribly wrong thing to do). In the journal it said something about how tired he was of always having to have sex with me in the mornings. The thing was, I didn't want to have sex either. I thought because he was hard, that meant I had to do it, and so I would iniate. I generally initiated when I thought someone wanted it, so that I wouldn't have to try and say no, and then be raped (even though this boy would have never ever raped me and I knew that). Reading his journal was the first time I realized that *I* could be the one who had power, and that I could be coercive even when I didn't want to be. This led me to really committ myself to reading about childhood sexual abuse, and looking at how my abuse history could make me do abusive things. Of course, it was a long task. I am still learning.

For me, it is important to remember that it is a long unlearning. I try and be really conscious, but sometimes can fall into old patterns when I least expect it. For awhile poly-amory was really important in trying to figure out my own sexuality and how to have healthy relationships, and sometimes I was good at it, and sometimes I used polyamory as an excuse to be dismissive of other people's feelings and needs. Reading Wendy-O-Matic's book <u>Redefining Our Relationships</u> was really useful to me in helping me figure out how to be ethical in my poly-amoury and not just to use it as a holier than thou manipulation tactic. Eventually I decided polyamory fed in to my over sexuilization of everyone I knew, and that I didn't want to be thinking that way about everyone. I wanted to be able to have clear friendships and clear boundries. It was really good for me to stop flirting and to figure out ways to connect with my friends that weren't sexual. I started to form much closer and more stable relationships with my friends, which has helped me learn about setting boundries and respecting boundries in all areas of my life.

I still struggle with always turning closeness into sexual feelings. I don't really blame myself for it, because I know that it comes from childhood abuse. I am trying to learn ways to be really upfront with my friends when I am trying to get physical, non-sexual comfort. I've found that even when it seems obvious, it's completely important to me to state from the beginning "I want to cuddle but don't want to do anything sexual." even when it is with my best friend and I have said it a hundred times before. I just almost always think that when someone touches me they want to have sex, and then I start responding to this assumed want. So stating what we are doing before hand helps.

There have been a couple times recently when I have been sleeping next to a new friend , who I felt pretty clearly like we wouldn't do anything but then we ended up doing sexual stuff that felt consensual. In both cases, I knew I should have talked about it as it was happening, and in both cases, I was older and so felt like it was my responsibility to bring it up, but I try not to beat myself up about it and I have made sure to talk to them later to make sure it was ok. These talks went really well.

POSITIVE CONSENT FOR DUDES WHO GET IT ON WITH DUDES

By Nick Riotfag

I could feel his hard-on pushing through the front of his scraggly cut-off shorts, against my own swelling crotch. I was in a bit of a daze, electrified by his arousal, thirsting for the salty taste of his neck, intoxicated by the friction of our sweaty bodies throbbing against each other. Finally, the making out ebbed to a point when we each paused to breathe, smile and make eye contact. I was hot, I was horny, I was ready for anything. Just ask, I'm yours, take anything you want from me.

With his arms around my shoulders, my ass in his lap, and our eyes locked, he opens his lips, pauses briefly in a smile, and murmurs in a gruff, soft, sexy voice:

> "I'd really love to fuck you. But... I want to get to know you first."

Huh?

Hold on, back up. Maybe I should provide some context.

So I'm a punk and an anarchist, and I also identify as a queer guy. Well, moreso as gay, but I sometimes sleep with non-male people. So maybe as 'bi', but the gender 'bi'nary is bullshit, and I feel much more identified with gay culture... or something. It's complicated. In any case, I've largely dated and slept with men, and I came out as queer and started participating in queer culture and activism before the punk/anarchist scene became my primary "home". In punk/anarchist scenes, I found the passionate political engagement, the unapologetic rejection of the mainstream, the fierce music, and the lifestyle that feels most compatible with my needs and desires. At the same time, even if I feel more at home at a squat or basement house show than a mainstream gay bar, it gets old having most of my anarchist male friends be totally straight, or "queer" in a way that doesn't involve dating men, least of all me. So I've always felt like I have one foot in each of these two very different scenes, and never really able to exist only in one without the other. This subcultural split has been the primary influence on the development of my sex life and how I experience and practice consent.

Some pretty significant differences exist between mainstream gay male sexual culture and that of punk/anarchist communities. As I think through my experiences, my desires, the norms and values I hold around sex, I can see how each community has shaped me differently. I recognize that each one has left me with certain things that I cherish, and certain things that I'm still struggling to overcome. Since I'm assuming, rightfully or not, that the readers of this DIY zine will probably have more context for punk/anarchist sexual culture than mainstream gay male sexual culture, I'm going to focus more on the latter, in hopes of showing some of the influences that have shaped me and some of the things that gay/bi male experiences can offer in learning about the complexities of consent. But first...

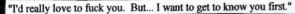

...Some thoughts on punk/anarchist sexual culture, consent, and queer men

In my opinion, the courageous kids who've pushed punk/anarchist scenes and communities to recognize sexual violence and transform norms around consent have begun to create a genuine shift in our shared culture. Over the past years of my involvement in this motley world of travelers and rabble-rousers, I've experienced significant qualitative differences in my sexual interactions with folks who've been socialized within these settings versus folks who haven't. Namely, I've found the punk/anarchist folks who've found their way into my pants to be notably more open to verbal consent and adept at practicing it (and finding it hot rather than mood-killing), less confined by gender stereotypes and narrow conceptions of what constitutes "sex", more comfortable with check-ins and communication about boundaries, and generally more compatible with my preferred style of getting it on.

Obviously, these are one person's experiences, and severe problems persist in every punk/anarchist community: continued belief in rape myths and survivor-blaming, "talking the talk" of feminism or consent while acting out the same shitty patterns, resistance to accountability or acknowledging abusive behavior, and innumerable other examples. Still, I've encountered so many steps in the right direction: the presence of consent-themed workshops and discussions at most radical gatherings, the widespread circulation of zines and writing about consent and positive sexuality, emerging reading/study/discussion

groups to focus on these issues in more depth, solid collective structures for community accountability in towns and at gatherings... these and many other signs point towards a shift in our whole way of thinking about sex and consent. In particular, absorbing and applying the feminist principle of politicizing the personal by insisting that these conversations must be PUBLIC and COMMUNITY-WIDE ones, rather than privatizing them as just our own personal business, indicates that we as punks and anarchists are striving to radically change the way we collectively and individually do sex and consent.

So why hasn't this trend translated into lots of hot punk dudes loving each other with verbal consent as an established norm? There are a couple of factors that I think play into this. For one, although there are certainly all kinds of exceptions to this, in general I've observed that predominantly folks socialized as women are leading this subcultural shift towards consent and challenging rape culture. Definitely many anarcha-feminist men are following along and participating actively in the movement to transform sexuality in more consensual directions, but I've encountered far fewer punk men who speak consent fluently than punk women, both sexually and in all sorts of interactions. So for me, as a guy who primarily sleeps with other guys, I much more often find myself in bed with someone who may have attended a consent workshop, but not someone who's led one. Until the norms around who takes seriously and gets involved in pro-consent organizing shift so that men see it as every bit as much of a priority, then I think that one outcome is that consent will remain under-emphasized amongst men who sleep with other men. Of course, this definitely doesn't mean that men should be usurping the leadership of pro-consent organizing and education away from women (as has happened in so many organizations and struggles), but rather than men should recognize our responsibility and our stake in promoting and modeling consensual behavior in all areas of our lives, and participate equally in working towards that change on a community level.

And another unfortunate and frustrating dynamic that helps explain why punk/anarchist consent norms haven't rubbed off on queer guys more is that many consent discussions, workshops, and such still frame sexual consent in really hetero terms. I've seen consent talked about as part of a man's responsibility in protecting women, almost some kind of weird chivalry, rather than a mutual responsibility to be practiced reciprocally between partners of any gender. Even gender-neutral presentations are usually based on hetero experiences, and almost never refer to specifically same-sex situations. Now, don't get me wrong - I recognize that a majority of sexual violence is committed by people socialized as men, and directed against people socialized as women. As such, it's important to target straight men with the messages that will encourage them to act more consensually. Likewise, it makes sense that the people who are designing and communicating these messages, who in my experience are primarily women whose partners are most often straight men, would see a clear interest in encouraging their current and potential partners to think more about consent. But here's the problem: the exclusion of queer relationships and same-sex sexuality from consent models means that we dude-loving dudes aren't hearing really important messages that could transform our sexuality in positive ways. And this has a lot of negative consequences.

Even in my own life and sexual relationships, I have felt as if careful verbal consent was more necessary or important in sexual situations with women than with men. Why? I think it's partly internalized homophobia- the idea that queer sex and relationships aren't as important or as "real" as hetero ones, thus don't require the same care and consideration between partners- and also partly because we as queer dudes almost never have pro-consent messages directed at us from the punk/anarchist world. I have had sexual interactions with men that felt considerably less communicative or consensual than what their other female partners would lead me to believe they should be. Likewise, I have seen kinds of harassment, objectification, and boundary-crossing directed from one man at another downplayed, laughed at, or even encouraged, when similar types of behavior directed by a man at a woman would be immediately condemned. Clearly, in spite of all of the positive progress in our community sexual norms around consent, we haven't always managed to make these shifts relevant to queer men – and as I'll talk about next, we don't get much pro-consent support from gay male mainstream messages about sex, either. Along with the norms I learned from punk/anarchist partners and our infrastructure of consent zines, workshops, discussions, etc, I learned a lot of separate and often very different lessons about consent and sex from gay/bi male sexual culture.

What I've learned from gay/bi male sexual culture

around HIV and other STDs and their transmission, and a historical sense of how incomprehensibly crushing the losses of the AIDS epidemic proved to gay and bi individuals and communities. I also learned to accept with minimal judgment the diversity of tastes and preferences people experience around sex, from BDSM to fetishes to sex with strangers or multiple partners. I learned that we could talk openly about intergenerational desire and sex without denial and sensationalizing. I learned that sex for sex's sake can be found almost anywhere, in bars, on the street, in parks, online, and just about anywhere that men congregate. And I learned that no one can define my desires but myself, that together with my queer comrades we can reject everything the "experts" try to say about us, and that free, open expression of sexuality can be a part of a revolutionary struggle to transform society from the, ahem, bottom up. (tee hee...)

At the same time, I learned of a sexual consumerism of the worst variety: a system mediated through internet sites and niche market pornography that reduced whole people to collections of characteristics, statistics, quantities. I learned that racist "preferences", body fascism, femme-phobia, and hierarchies of cock size were accepted as neutral, apolitical, and beyond critique, because "we're just in to what we're in to, that's all." I learned to define myself in terms of my sexuality, with affirmation of my identity and self-worth derived from the number and type of sexual partners I acquired. In other words, I learned from gay male sexual culture some of the most hurtful aspects of conventional masculinity in terms of sex, on top of those same messages from dominant straight media and culture to which most male-socialized people have been subjected. This contradictory legacy I've inherited from the sexual culture of gay and bi men shapes my desires and how I experience them, and lays the groundwork for what constitutes consent for me.

Gay/bi men and verbal consent

It's an uncomfortable but consistent part of my experience: amongst gay and bi men, I have not very often found partners who prefer verbal consent. On the one hand, something sounds frustratingly authoritarian in the declaration some anarchists I know have made that "any sex without verbal consent is assault", when the norms of one of the most central sexual subcultures in my life almost never condone or appreciate that style of interaction. At the same time, finding queer men who appreciate and practice the style of verbal consent and sexual communication that works best for me has been one of the most affirming, energizing, and relieving (not to mention HOT) aspects of my sexual history. The rarity of it helps let me know when I do find someone who likes it the way I do that they're probably someone pretty special. But why do so few of the men-loving men, at least the ones I've known and been with, practice and appreciate verbal consent during sex? I can think of a few reasons.

One is that for many men who enjoy sex with men, that pleasure is fraught with guilt, secrecy, denial, and other painful emotions forced on them by the conditioning of a homophobic society. As such, many guys find it INCREDIBLY hard to speak the truth of their longings. Some find it repulsive to say out loud, or to hear someone say, the acts they do or long for. Particularly for closeted or straight-identified guys, verbalizing desire would mean taking on gayness in a way that they can't handle, so communicating with body language and acts, often through the filter of alcohol or drugs, provides the only means they have of living out their fantasies. Even men who are more comfortable with their same-sex desire and behavior have learned that their partners aren't always, and have found it more sexually promising (or even physically safer) to simply act and leave their unspeakable acts unspoken. Especially with sexual acts that are stigmatized more heavily for being "feminine", such as getting fucked anally, a verbal acknowledgment of one's desire can feel humiliating in a way that detracts from the pleasure of the act itself.

Another factor that diminishes the importance of verbal consent is the fact that a significant amount of gay sex is negotiated through online hookup sites or public cruising, both of which involve engaging only for a limited amount of time on an explicitly sexual basis. If I chat with someone on Manhunt.net or we make eyes in a park, we both know that if I head over to his apartment, it's for one reason only. As a result, many assume that consent has been pre-emptively communicated through someone's very presence. In many cases, especially online, the participants agree upon their desired roles or activities beforehand, leaving even less room for uncertainty. Of course, a world of nuance exists beyond the fact of mutual desire that complicates consent, but in a sexual culture that commonly involves brief, exclusively sexual, pre-arranged interactions, verbal negotiation in the moment is not always as central as in other sexual settings.

Still another reason why verbal consent isn't more prominent amongst men who have sex with men lies in the fact that gay male sexual culture involves some reflections of the dominant culture's sexual socialization around masculinity and desirability. "Real" men (who, of course, we who love men are supposed to desire above all others) are those who take charge, who know what they want and get it: active = masculine. Many gay men I know say that they long for a man who will be aggressive with them, take charge sexually and sweep them off their feet. There's something suspiciously feminine about asking first, about not claiming to effortlessly mind-read your partners and take charge to enact their desires on you, about being careful to listen to someone else's needs and boundaries. And nothing is less sexy, in a frequently misogynist and femme-phobic gay male culture, then that which is feminine. Since gay and bi men have our masculinity questioned, devalued, and denied by the dominant hetero culture around us all the time, many of us attempt to compensate by rejecting all things female or feminine. Sadly, this often manifests in hurtful, sexist ways, ranging from outright misogyny and disrespect towards/exclusion of women to chauvinistically rejecting any partner whose conventional masculinity isn't up to snuff. In reality, gay and bi men desire men with a wide range of gender characteristics - we femmes know that we can still get laid pretty often, too, in spite of their "straight-acting, masc only" bluffs! However, in terms of what's valued or socially acceptable, the norms of conventional masculinity dictate the standards, and one part of that involves pressure to be a sexual mind-reader and please one's partner without having to ask. Gay and bi men play both sides of that dynamic, both the butch top stud who aims to impress with action, not words, and the guy who's turned off by anyone who doesn't just take charge but stops to ask and check in.

Positive consent for hot man-on-man action

So in light of all these barriers to verbal consent, what does a hot man-to-man encounter with solid, positive consent look like? Well, it looks different for everyone, but for me at least, there are some key components. There are lots of zines and essays that lay out the most important basics – knowing your boundaries beforehand; asking at each new level of sexual activity; acknowledging nonverbal cues and body language as well as verbal cues; everyone should be sober enough to be clear on what's going on; and all that important stuff. What I want to add are just a few other things formulated with queer dudes specifically in mind. Pretty much all of these are relevant to people of any gender and sexual orientation, but they come out of my specific experience as a guy getting it on with guys. So when I think about hooking up with a cutie, here's part of what I'm thinking:

RESPECT YOURSELF

Cheesy as it may sound, this is by far and away the most important part. Queers who love and respect ourselves are more likely to think about, decide on, and stand up for our boundaries; more likely to insist on safer sex; and more likely to be able to walk away from any encounter that seems sketchy knowing that we will be able to find love, affirmation, and sexual release elsewhere. It is so hard to know what consent means, let alone give it and receive it, without first believing that we are WORTH being afforded the respect of consent. So please, take the time to learn to love yourself – you're worth it!

NEGOTIATE SAFER SEX FIRST

Don't fuck around with your health. Before you start fretting over positions or roles, cover your bases around safer sex. Know your limits, communicate them clearly, and don't compromise – even if they're reeeeally hot, even if they claim can't get off with a condom, even if they won't let you blow them if you insist on a barrier, no matter what. Keep condoms with you or handy at all times when there's a possibility of having sex – don't rely on your partner(s) to have them. Get tested regularly, and if you have an ongoing partner, make sure that they do, too. Don't assume your partner(s) HIV or other STD/STI status, and don't assume that they'll tell you the full truth. Remember that acts that are safe for HIV aren't always safe for other painful or even incurable diseases (syphilis, herpes, etc), and that even if you're already HIV positive, staying healthy means avoiding other infections. Make sure that you're consenting just to the sex, not to an infection or disease that could last a lifetime.

ASK WHAT STYLE OF CONSENT THEY LIKE

Truth is, some people just don't like verbal consent. It may be for some of the reasons that I discussed above about gay/bi male sexual culture; it may be because they haven't challenged some of the crappy mainstream conditioning they've received from media, pop culture, and so forth; it may be for totally different and valid reasons that you don't have context to understand. In any case, the important thing is for you to know what works for you- if you can't have a positive experience without clear, consistent verbal consent, then maybe you shouldn't hop into bed with someone who isn't willing to try it. So ask up front, gauge how somebody prefers to communicate their desires, preferences, and boundaries – and be clear enough on your own to say no thanks if theirs don't line up with yours.

FUCK OUT OF THE CLOSET

Here's a suggestion, which is sure to be controversial, but comes from my experience: it might not be worth the trouble to hook up with guys who aren't comfortable enough with their sexuality to be able to say what they want. Making it with straight guys may be hot, and it may give your ego a boost knowing you've bedded the unbeddable, but in my experience, in most cases it's not worth it. Save yourself the trouble and hook up with folks who are comfortable enough with themselves and their desires to be able to talk about them openly. It's not important what identity or label they use for themselves; what's important is if they're able to communicate directly about what they want, without having to be wasted to do it, or blundering their way through awkward sex silently. It's also safer - watch out for rough trade, a.k.a. dudes who'll let you suck them off but then work themselves into a homophobic rage at you after orgasm.

FIGHT HOMOPHOBIA AND HETEROSEXISM

One of the major barriers to being able to love freely and consensually is the oppressive systems set up by our society to make us hate ourselves and our desires. There are tons of rad ways to fight them, though! First and foremost, we can come out and live openly as who we are – every person makes it a little easier for everyone else. We can organize for the same rights, acknowledgement, and dignities afforded to straight people, but we don't have to assimilate into their norms of monogamy, marriage, and nuclear families. We can challenge the blatant and subtle ways that queer people get excluded – for example, demanding that consent workshops and discussions have gender neutral frameworks and include queer-specific examples. We can provide space for queer youth to exist freely, acknowledge them as sexual beings without being exploitative or objectifying, and serve as mentors and positive role models. And fuck homophobic religious assholes – we can refuse to tolerate fundamentalist bullshit that denies our humanity under the guise of the Bible, the word of some god or some preacher, or some idiotic sense of what's "natural". All of these things are interrelated parts of how we can transform our culture to create more space to openly acknowledge and ask for the things we want sexually, which will lay the groundwork for pro-consent sexual norms.

NEGOTIATE ONLINE

For better or for worse, a lot of sex between men gets arranged on the internet. Some think this is in part because the constraints of a homophobic society prevent us from meeting each other as openly as straight people can; whether or not that's the case, this is the reality we're dealing with, and we can take advantage of it to promote consent. Talking through a computer screen can lessen the fear of rejection, desire to appear coy or indirect, and other things that make talking about consent harder. And however shitty the consumerism of online sex may be, the vast array of postings can serve as a reminder that if we don't feel comfortable with someone, there will be other options for sexual release. By posting our preferences in an ad or profile, and chatting with someone beforehand specifically about the kind of sex we want to have, we can set up whatever norms of consent feel best for us. The risk of this, of course, is that pre-arranged agreements for what to do and how to do it with someone may lead them (or you) to believe that there's no need to check in verbally, to be aware of body language and nonverbal cues, to make space to pause or stop completely if something doesn't feel right. But if we choose to go the internet route, we can use it as a lower-pressure way to set up consent practices beforehand that reflect our own needs and ideals.

THINK ABOUT CONSENT AND GENDER

For me, good consent requires being aware of, and rejecting, gender roles in sexual settings. I know that I can't feel solid in the consensuality of a sexual interaction when everything - from who initiates to what acts we do together and who's penetrated by what - is determined by the gender role conditioning that strangles us, rather than by our own desires, needs, preferences, and boundaries. The impact of this socialization shows itself most clearly in cross-sex interactions, but pops up in same-sex adventures, too. For instance, if a same-sex couple includes a more masculine or butch partner, gender conventions may dictate that that person shouldn't be penetrated, or should take the lead, or should act in a certain way based on gendered dynamics. This is understandable, in a mainstream heterosexual culture that conceives of sex so narrowly that it asks same-sex couples "who's the man" or "who's the woman"; it's hard to avoid absorbing the constant denial and ridicule of our right to sexual and gender self-determination. In any case, regardless of the gender of the partner who's hot for me, and regardless of whether I'm wearing a pink mini-skirt or overalls and boots (or both!), for sex to be fully consensual for me I need to be confident that everyone involved has some consciousness of how gender impacts our expectations about what we should do, and that we've all chosen to reject those imposed expectations in favor of focusing on our actual desires.

(Of course, sometimes our desires may fall along starkly gendered lines, in ways that may feel uncomfortable to self-defined radicals who love to fuck with gender but can't seem to fuck without it. We can get stuck in guilt and reject ourselves for our illicit desires, just as christian anti-sex bullshit wants us to, or we can stubbornly defend our most conventional longings without regards to the patriarchal and abusive patterns they may seem to uphold. Between this rock and hard place, the only way I've been able to find a place that feels good is just to talk with my partners as honestly as I can about my desires and how I feel about them and how they do or don't relate to my politics, and go from there. The point for me isn't to get our desires to conform to our political aspirations- desire will never submit to being civilized into such tidy ideological constructs. The point, as far as I see it, is to set out towards being as consensual and as critical and honest and as self-loving as possible. If there's any beauty we can find between our quaking bodies in this fucked up culture, it might be along those paths.)

Positive, full, life-affirming consent for me also requires an awareness of the role that all sex in general, and individual sexual encounters specifically, play in my life as a whole. At different times, I have longed for, pursued, and engaged in various kinds of sex for a litany of different reasons: horniness, profound love and emotional connection, loneliness, curiosity, affectionate friendship, a sense of adventure and daring, boredom, indifference in the face of another's strong longing, a desire to please or to avoid hurting feelings, a need for resources controlled by someone else (rent money, a place to crash for the night, status or prestige), the pressure of masculine socialization, to impress someone, to flaunt social norms, to sustain a lagging relationship, to piss off a third party, to avoid awkward silences... and those are just the reasons of which I'm consciously aware! Can I be confident that I (or my partner[s], for that matter) are choosing freely and eagerly to have sex if I'm/we're not conscious of the motivations behind our desires and choices? Of course, it's possible to get swallowed into feeling so anxious about our motivations that we over-analyze everything and never muster the courage for a kiss! Still, while avoiding that extreme, I've found that it's crucial for me to have ongoing dialogue with others, and most importantly myself, in non-sexual situations about how sex and sexuality fits into my present life. That way, when I'm stricken with longing or presented with opportunity, I can make a decision based in a more holistic sense of myself, which more accurately reflects how I feel about a particular encounter.

This of course relates to people of any gender and sexual orientation, but it stems in part from my recognizing the pressure on gay men to define ourselves as part of a community through sex. I've wanted to have sex at times to shore up my sense of gayness, to affirm the feeling of connection to community that I get through my identification as queer. But what I'm really longing for at those times isn't actually sex, but the warm feelings of inclusion and affirmation that come from being a part of a community. That realization shook me up a bit, and prompted me ask myself difficult questions about whether or not sex I had based off of those desires was truly consensual on a deeper level. The important thing, I think, is that now I have a whole new level on which I think about consent, one that considers the whole context of myself and my life in my sexual decision-making. Yeah, it's complicated, but it's important, and ultimately really positive for me.

****

Anyway, back to me and E. I smiled and exhaled, feeling more relief than I had realized, more than made sense in that hot and horny moment before having had the time to look back on it and appreciate just what that statement meant to me. I liked E because he was attracted to me, because he was a flirt and a slut and seductively charming. But whether or not I would have anticipated it, I liked it WAY, way more when he affirmed that he wanted me to be more than just a body to get himself off on- he wanted to experience a connection with me that included but went beyond just our bodies. Let me be clear- this is not to pass judgment on anyone whose preferred type of sexuality is much more anonymous or less connected on non-physical levels. It's just an acknowledgement that my ideas of consent had to expand when I admitted that even with this gorgeous guy to whom I was quite attracted and with whom I would have gladly committed a litany of perversities, consent meant more than just getting horny and going with it. It meant for me in that moment a mutual recognition and affirmation of one another's humanity, one that truly created the space for me - or him - to say no, or yes, or let's wait, or any number of other things. It meant listening to my body as well as my heart as well as my brain, and recognizing that I can't separate out those parts of me as if I'm not a whole, integrated person.

So that's what I mean by positive consent for dudes who get it on with dudes! I welcome any thoughts or feedback on this article at xriotfagx@riseup.net.

Best wishes for a world full of hot queer loving,
Nick

back safely

I'm in what I refer to as a hyper-consensual relationship. We talk about consent and try to practice consent when we're in bed, when we're not in bed, through letters, over the phone....it weaves throughout the fabric of our relationship. It is the forum for our processing, where we get to see how our relationship is growing, changing, becoming more and more intimate. We talk about language - what language empowers us, what language we feel comfortable with. I feel comfortable saying breasts, she doesn't. She feels comfortable saying vag, I don't. It's ok to have two sets of vocabulary, one for my body and one for hers. We talk about phrasing, about the connotations of things. We try to say "Do you want me to" instead of "Can I"...we *can* do a lot of things, and they might not be particularly uncomfortable...but do we *want* it? We struggle, with an imbalance of initiations - the conditioning we've received that makes it challenging sometimes to not only find and use our voices to express desires, but to even be in touch with those desires in the first place. The other night I asked her over the phone if she likes the way I touch her body when we kiss, because I'm not always sure. She said yes but that she needed me to check in more, ask for consent about specific touches before I do them. These were things I used to ask about, used to never assume. Part of me was so happy and relieved she told me, told me that these things I was doing needed to be worked on. But part of me wanted to cry and not touch her again, scared I had hurt her and I couldn't take that back. Part of me hated myself. This is what we struggle with... negotiating, learning together, accepting that we are in a process and not perfect...accepting that we are just trying, trying to be in a relationship in a way that hasn't been modeled for us, culturally...a relationship where we're moving beyond love & good intentions, moving into processing, communication, vulnerability, practice...

Everything escalated slowly and she would stop kissing me and look me in the eyes and say, "How are ya doing?" She would stop to check in with me even though I always said yes, and it made me feel like I was respected. It made me feel like I was safe. Because in the back of my mind, I knew that if, for some reason, I should stop feeling comfortable and if, for some reason, I didn't feel like I could speak up, she would ask again and there would be the space to back out or slow things down. I didn't feel trapped, the way I had always felt before, like "I've gone this far, now there's no way to get out of it." She gave me a choice at each new level, and just because we had already done something before didn't mean she didn't ask for permission before doing it again.

Consent can be so fucking scary because you're opening yourself to up rejection. You're creating a safe space, a space where your partner can say no. But what's so hot, so empowering, so fucking amazing about consent is that the yes's really become yes's. The first time you hear no, it validates all the yes's. The first time you hear no, it's not really a rejection, a failure of any kind. It's a reassurance that when you hear yes, it's a yes, and they'll tell you otherwise when it's not. The yes's become erotic and the no's are signs of the safety and the trust that have been built, that consent actually works, that what you are doing is worth all the work, is right.

I assume everyone I come in contact with is a survivor. If they tell me otherwise at some point, then great, but I'd rather be conscious of my behavior than to hurt someone and find out after the fact that it could have been avoided with some simple consent practices. I've learned to ask people if I can give them hugs. I ask children if I can pick them up. I ask a crying friend if they want to be held, if they feel comfortable if I hold their hand. I have a friend who is a massage therapist. "The first rule of massage is to always obtain consent first," he said. "But I realized," he continued, "that it's not just about massage...that I have to apply the principles of consent to every interaction I have in my life..." I think about what he said when I sit next to strangers on the bus, when I help people at work, when I talk with friends. Consent isn't inherently sexual. It's about communication, about working towards creating safe spaces. I want intimate, private experiences to be safe, but I want to feel safe in public, too. Thinking about consent in all of my interactions makes me feel like I'm making a start on some level, doing my part to make that happen.. When we practice consent we create our own safe spaces, and then see where those spaces overlap with others'.

This was my introduction to an experiential understanding of the practice of consent, of what it really feels like and why it's so important: I remember sitting on the edge of the bed, making out, but making out really sweetly, with soft kisses, and I remember thinking to myself "this is the best part"...and then I remember jumping off the bed, pacing, my heart pounding, scared to death, with a pit in my stomach that felt like it was swallowing me alive. I felt like a little kid. I started muttering shit to myself and it just got worse and worse. I tried to force it, to go back and just keep going. I couldn't stay in my body, couldn't keep myself from being pulled into the vortex that left me curled up in a ball under the covers crying. I couldn't open my mouth and I couldn't look at her. I wanted to tell her that it wasn't her, that she didn't do anything, that it wasn't her fault, that I loved her - but I couldn't say anything. She sat there for a minute and then I heard her say, "Do you want me to stay here with you or do you need space?" I couldn't answer so she made it a yes or no question and she asked again, "Do you want me to stay here with you?" I nodded my head yes underneath the protective layers of bedding. "Can I touch you?" she asked and I nodded yes again and felt her hand on my shoulder. "You're okay," she started saying softly, "everything's okay, you're safe...you're safe...you're safe..." She asked if she could hold me and I nodded yes, so she curled around me and held me softly and I started shaking and crying. She stopped asking me questions and just let me cry and held me. When I was done crying I moved the blankets down off my face and I turned around and faced her. I wouldn't look into her eyes but she held my head softly until I did and she asked me where I was. "Are you here?" "It's safe now, everything's okay," she said. I had never disassociated and come back before. I had always had to sleep it off, wake up the next day groggy and confused. But we had talked before about triggers, about how sometimes I dissociated and what that meant for me, about what I needed when that happened. We had sat there together and read the *Support* zine, we went through the questionnaire about consent in the beginning of it...we had prepared for experiences like this. She practiced what we had talked about, and it was the first time anyone had ever been able to bring me back, and bring me back safely. ✐

numbers

I have never been able to figure out a way to talk comfortably about consent.

I think I am pretty good about asking other people, but figuring out a way to explain whether or not I want to be doing something is pretty impossible. I mean, if I want to be doing something, it's usually fine, but if I don't, or especially if I'm unsure, it's impossible. If someone asks, "is this ok," I always say "yes." Everything is "ok" I mean, I can survive anything, right? So even the best of intentions don't usually work for me, and just the words like "do you like this?" or "do you want me to be doing this?" they are triggering, or even if they're not specifically triggering, they make me doubt myself - like "Oh, I thought I wanted this, but do I? What if I don't? shit. How do I know for sure?" So generally when people ask me for consent it not only ruins the mood I'm working so hard to maintain, but it triggers me, then I have to try and navigate wheter or not I'm going to be able to get out of the trigger, stop thinking so much and get back to just feeling good. And if they notice me flinching or withdrawing for a second and they stop and want to tqlk about it, then it is just over, and may be I don't want it to be over, I just want to be able to work through it myself and forget.

So I've never really known what to do.
There are some things that have worked
- like talking beforehand about what
I need - like being held after sex. And
asking them not to ask me things like
"how was it for you". There are just too
many words and sentences that are
triggering for me. But I love sex and
want to be able to do it. I want

to be able to be asked for consent and to give
 consent. If people don't even try, then that's
 frustrating too.

So, talking beforehand, and also trying to figure
out ways to talk about what's happened during sex,
but later. like when we are not in bed. and trying
to figure out ways for them to not get freaked out
if I admit to faking it or having a flashback or
just not wanting to do something. It's important
for me to be able to talk about it later, because
1 can't usually talk about it at the time, but
that usually makes people feel like shit and feel
guilty and then question every move they make, and
they feel like they can't get anything right and
1 have to take all initiative and give so much
reasurance, and that makes me never feel like
doin' it, and that sucks too.

One of the things that happens a lot is that I
am really sexual in the beginnings of relationships
but when they get more serious or when they have
been going on for awhile more things start to come
up. My last partner came up with an idea. 1 have
to say that the fact that he came up with an idea
instead of me having to do it, helped so much! He
came up with a number system He would ask me 1-6
We worked together to come up with what the numbers
stood for.

1. I feel like being held. No sex. Nothing. Not
   even sexual energy.
2. I want kissing but nothing past that. No
   moving against me in a sexual way.
3. I want to kiss and might be open to other stuff
   too.
4. I want to do stuff, but check back in a lot
   as we go.
5. I want to do stuff, and don't want much checking
   in, just check in before doing anything with the
   downthere parts and chēck in if you feel like I
   might be feeling weird.
6. Let's do it!

Something about the number system took the
weight off things. It made it more easy and a
little bit funny. I was totally able to say 2,
where as I would never say "I want to kiss right
now but nothing else". Saying those words would
make me feel totally guilty where as saying "two"
just felt like fact.
It didn't always work perfectly, but it was way
easier for both of us.

Embodied Consent

The information that you receive from your body in the form of sensations, feelings, and intuition is key to the process of making choices. Survivors learn to override their feelings and acquiesce to others' wishes. I want to invite you back into your body now. From inside your own body, you can decide what you want sexually based on your own needs, desires, and values. I call this embodied consent.

The first step in embodied consent is noticing your own body sensations and signals. What are you feeling in your chest, your pelvis, your stomach? When you are doing something that you want to do, when your insides are saying "yes," how do you know this? For example, one survivor I worked with said her stomach relaxes and she gets a warm sensation there when she knows it is okay for her to go ahead. Another survivor reported that she felt an openness and warmth in her pelvis and a connection to her voice and throat when she felt a "yes." Check this out for yourself. How do you know when your body says "yes"?

Conversely, what signals and sensations appear in your body when you do not want to engage in a certain sexual experience? How do you know when it is not feeling right anymore? Another survivor reported: "I start to feel panicky in my chest and want to pull away physically. I usually try to talk myself into sexual contact, telling myself, 'what's the bid deal? Nothing bad is happening.' Then in I don't listen to my body, I usually check out and have sex without being there." When you do not want to be sexual in some way, you may notice your breathing getting short, your stomach getting tight, or your body wanting to pull away. Pay attention. This is *you* communicating to you. What sensations in your body communicate a "no" to you?

And what about maybe? Sometimes there are a number of seemingly contradictory feelings happening in your body at once. You may feel sexually turned on in your hips and vulva, and feel pulled away in your chest. You may feel a warmth in your solar plexus, indicating go-ahead, and be afraid or tight in your throat. What do you do then?

Actually, experiencing contradictory feelings is familiar territory for most survivors. Consent then becomes a matter of distinguishing what sensations are what. One workshop participant noted, "I feel the consent to be sexual in my belly, it is a settled, sure sensation, and I can feel anxious in my chest at the same time. I am anxious when I am getting close to someone. I can count on this happening. It does not mean I do not want to be sexual. It just means I am feeling scared while I am being sexual." Another survivor shared, "I usually stop having sex when my stomach gets tight. I see now, though, that my stomach being tight is me feeling stressed about being turned on. It was so awful to get turned on during the sexual molestation that my body still tries not to do it. If I just relax and acknowledge my stomach and the fear there, I can go right on being sexual. My stomach being tight does not mean I do not want to have sex."

Sometimes we make choices about sex in our heads, because it seems like a good idea, seems to make sense, when we may be feeling something entirely different in our bodies.

You can end up feeling used, angry, or self-loathing after such a decision.

Consent does not always *feel* comfortable, easy, and joyous. Sometimes a consensual experience can bring up sadness, anger, or feelings of abandonment. It is important to learn the difference between experiencing feelings and wanting to stop what you are doing. You can do this by paying attention to your body and learning its language.

FROM SURVIVORS GUIDE TO SEX

Desiring Consent
By Lee Hunter

For a couple of years I co-facilitated workshops about consent and got to hear a lot of people talk about how they bring up consent and talk about sex. It is my hope to avoid wasting all the interactions I had over the years by conveying some of the wisdom that I learned from listening to people talk about consent. These conversations were really awesome and helped me learn to define consent and my boundaries. Thanks to everyone I have ever been in a workshop with! Talking about consent can be difficult at first, creating awkward situations. But as you continue talking about your desires, it becomes easier and easier, and for most a prerequisite to any sex that occurs.

Consent is a term that people have to define for themselves and people define consent in a number of different ways. Here are some examples from past workshops:

"Consent is never assumed, consent isn't defined the same way by everybody, consent is verbal, consent can be nonverbal including body language, consent is never assumed with strangers OR long term partners, consent is an ongoing process at each new stage, consent is only possible when healthy communication is possible."

"Consent is knowing and respecting my personal and sexual boundaries and learning, knowing, and respecting the boundaries of my partner."

And another definition from the now defunct *Blackthorn(*Issue 3, 2004), a paper from Portland, OR.

"Consent is hard to define because there are many different levels of communication (body language, flirting/innuendo, conversing, etc.) The only way to be certain that there is consent is through explicit verbal communication: "Can i touch you here?" "yes/no you can/'t touch me there."

There is no set definition of consent. Developing your own definition of consent is an important part of the process of defining your desires and learning how to communicate them to others.

Healthy communication is a huge part of consent. Consent does not have to be a process that involves stopping and asking the person that you are with if they are okay all of the time or if it is okay if you touch them on the breast or on the genitals—unless of course it needs to be that way. People communicate about sex in different ways, some are more verbal than others, while some find talking in the heat of the moment to be a real turn off. The important part is for you to figure out what method works the best for you and the person or people you're with. Do you like it when someone asks before they kiss you or touch you in sexy ways or would you prefer to have a conversation and negotiate the kind of sex you would like to have prior to even getting to the sex?

Figuring out what you like and don't like is a huge part of defining your boundaries and through the definitions of your boundaries it is possible to consent to different activities. Boundaries are applicable to all aspects of your life. They are the barriers we develop and articulate in order to understand why we say yes or no. Sometimes boundaries get pushed and occasionally they get crossed. When a boundary is crossed it can be a liberating experience or a violating one, depending on the situation. In many cases, the act of boundary crossing is the source of a lot of the sexual assault that occurs. In other cases, you learn that something you didn't think turned you on, in fact does. I cannot stress how important it is to know your boundaries. A good way to figure out what your boundaries are is talking with your friends and lovers about what you like, what's happened to you in the past, and what your future fantasies are.

Boundaries, like consent, are not fixed. Consent may be given at the beginning of the night and taken away by the end of the night. There is no set of rules about consent, as there is no one definition of consent. Defining consent is a personal process, as you think about the situations you don't ever want to be in again and the kinds of places you want to go with your sex life. Unfortunately, many of the people reading this zine have probably experienced some sort of sexual assault in their lives and that complicates things as well.

For those of you who are reading this who have not experienced sexual assault first hand, I would like to leave you with a couple of things to think about. Many people have been assaulted, not just *women.* First I'd like to encourage people to talk about sex and abuse history prior to sleeping with each other. Sometimes people are not ready or don't want to talk about assault histories, so don't push a subject that a person doesn't want to talk about, this should be obvious. Second, people who have been abused usually, not always, have triggers. When these triggers are tripped, the person will checkout of reality and probably go somewhere else in their heads. Physically this can look many different ways: a sudden quiet when there had been a lot of noise, going still or corpse like, or staring off into space. Everyone's triggers look different and this is where prior conversations can really help. Sometimes there are certain actions that will cause the trigger to go off, like being grabbed from behind or feeling like you're getting smothered and you are more likely to be aware of when a person is being triggered if you've talked about it ahead of time. As far as I can tell most humans are not mind readers and not always as observant as we'd like them to be, so talking about sexual history can really help.

My suggestion is to learn how to be verbal about your needs. As a person who has been sexually assaulted, it took me a long time to learn how to talk about my abuse history and learn how to have a sex-posi attitude and now no one can take that back from me. I am not a victim. I have learned my strengths and how to fulfill my desires and I am pro-sex. And as far as I can tell, everyone has the ability to feel this way; it's not always easy, but it's possible! Sometimes therapy can really help and I say this with the knowledge that therapy can take many different forms. I found that one of the most important things for me was finding other friends to talk about sex with and learning how to share my experiences with others. Learn your triggers and how to articulate them, if you have them, it can really help in having healthier sex and helps to define boundaries.

Another issue that has come up a lot is consent and gender. While talking to many of male friends, it has come to my attention that in the heterosexual world particularly, consent is thought to be a male directed action. That men must always initiate sex and women say yes or no. I must admit that I am always in shock about this idea that women are not supposed to or don't initiate, but this assumption really does come up a lot. I'd like to just remind everyone that consent is not a gendered activity, in the het or queer scene. Consent is every individual's responsibility and communicating about sex is important no matter where you fall in the gender spectrum.

At this point, most of the discussions that I have about consensual sex are self- initiated. I have been practicing this kind of dialogue for long enough that I no longer find it embarrassing to talk about my sexual desires and boundaries with another person. Whether they are a one-night stand or a potential longer term lover, everyone gets the same speech. And it turns out that lots of people find it really hot to talk about what kind of sex they are going to be having before it happens. In most cases prior negotiations about sex have really worked out for me. This is not a fail proof method, but my success rate has been startling.

Depending on the kind of sex you like to have, informed verbal consent is absolutely necessary before any type of sexual activity is gonna happen. If you are into kinky sex, then chance are you've already learned a lot about consent. Due to the kind of sex involved in BDSM, that scene has some of the best definitions of consent and practical ways of discussing sex that I have seen. When you are participating in activities that can be potentially physically harmful and cause hospitalization, it is absolutely necessary to have a negotiation and consent process. As long as sex is consensual, there is no limit to the things you can do and places you can explore.

Alcohol and drugs are not a great combination for consensual sex. There are many people who do not believe it is possible to have consensual sex if you have been drinking or doing drugs. This is an open question for me, since in my experience it has depended on the situation. However, it may be the case that an individual is not capable of making healthy decisions under the influence, and this needs to be taken into consideration when thinking about one's own boundaries and how to define them. It is unfortunate that sex creates so many uncomfortable and awkward situations for people, making it feel so necessary to pull out the goggles of intoxication. Our culture does not encourage us to communicate about our bodies and how we relate sexually to one another, much less about whether we are having healthy, fun, fulfilling sex with each other. It's a shame that so much pain comes from something that can be so damn fun.

Here is a situation in which consent worked out really well. One night I was out drinking by myself at a bar and I ran into a couple of friends. There was a person that I had not met before and I thought to myself, "Delicious, I'd like to make-out with that person." Several beers later, we were kissing in the parking lot out back. I invited him back to my house on the condition that we would not sleep with each other due to the fact we had just met and we were both pretty drunk. He agreed and the next thing I knew we were in my bed, making out and groping. At a certain point it seemed like we would be breaking our verbal agreement, then he asked, "Do you think we should take this any farther?" I replied, "No, I don't think so, we agreed we weren't gonna fuck before you came here." He said, "Yeah, you are right." And that was the end of it. We kissed some more and fell asleep.

I like this example, because it reminds me that consent is totally attainable and I'd like to think it's possible for everyone. I also used this example because (let's just go ahead and admit it) the fact is that a lot of people get drunk and fuck each other. In many cases the sex that is had is not consensual. To be clear for anyone who is hazy on this fact, having sex with people who are passed out is called rape! For some reason, I have heard a lot of people deliberate about this type of situation, which happens more than I can tolerate. If you have been assaulted, please talk to people that you trust and figure out a way to deal with the trauma—but survivor tactics are a topic for another essay.

Even though consent seems awkward and sometimes silly, it is a really great process that can enable lots of great sex. Healthy communication skills are necessary, as we learn to discuss the topic of sex with each other and become comfortable with the topic. Learning what your boundaries are and how to communicate them is one of the first steps to forming healthier sex relationships, regardless of whether you are negotiating with a one-night stand or a long-term partner. Boundaries can change over time and consent can be revoked at anytime. But most of all, I hope that you are all having lots and lots of really hot, steamy, consensual sex!

Below are notes and discussion questions that we use to facilitate a workshop and discussion on communication and sex. We usually do a 15 minute intro to give people a sense of what we want to bring up and lay out some guidelines for the discussion. Then we do a puppet show to get people thinking about what communication around consent (including talking about STIs) looks like - when it's done well and when it's not done or when communication could be better. It's a humorous way to bring up elements of consent that can be difficult to talk about: intoxication, gender, hook ups vs. long term relationships... This leads into a group discussion. Below are some of the questions we use during the discussion. This is not a fixed outline - we don't try to bring up everything listed. It's useful as a way of guiding our conversation and having questions to help prompt discussion. We do that for about half an hour and then break into small groups to have more in-depth discussions and so more people can participate. We encourage people to talk about and come up with practical steps for how we can improve communication around consent in our own lives. Then, we come back together to share ideas from the small groups and look at our growing definitions of consent. Want the script for the puppet show or to talk more about the workshop? Email us at: downtherehealth at mutualaid.org.

Take care, Down There Health Collective

CONSENT – Sex and Communication

When people come in ask them to write down their personal definition of consent, add to this definition during the workshop as new thoughts and ideas occur to you.

I. INTRO TO COLLECTIVE AND OUR GOALS FOR THE WORKSHOP (10 MIN)

INTRO:
- Introduce the Collective.
- *See No, Speak No, Hear No* zine sparked our interest and internal discussions about consent.
- Share personal story or goal, why we're interested in this workshop

OVERVIEW OF THE WORKSHOP / AGENDA
- Consent and communication could be week long workshops in themselves. Facilitators will be moving the discussions along so we can touch on a variety of areas.

GOALS:

- Redefine consent – to question and broaden our ideas. Defining what consent means to each of us.
- Transform society to one based on consent and not coercion; applies to other aspects of life.
- Equip you (and us) with examples of how to be more proactive in creating safe consensual spaces. Focus on communicating, being upfront, and being positive. (Will not focus on assault)

- Discuss dynamics / factors that might be influencing how we give or receive consent – age, power, relationships, etc.
- Look honestly at patterns in our own relationships
- Improve your sex life! We think that consent can be hott and liberating.
- Create a space for a healthy conversation. Provoke thought and further discussion. There aren't many places where there are right or wrong answers. There will be a lot of open and unanswered questions.

SUPPORT PERSON PRESENTS

- This workshop is exciting because it's an opportunity to work through ideas, construct how we want things to be, propose ideals.
- Discussion could trigger difficult memories or feelings for those who identify as having abuse or assault in their history
- And potentially for all of us, because we do not live in a culture of consent and may have had negative experiences of boundary violations that we don't think of in concrete terms.
- Please be sure to check in with yourself and be aware of your emotional state. Just

  because this discussion is happening now does not mean that you need to deal with this stuff now.
- Feel free to leave at any time, if you want to get some water or go to the bathroom, and come back, or not come back, its okay. Take a friend with you if you want. And please try to be aware of your friends too, and check in about how they are feeling.
- I am going to sit by the door and am here if anyone wants to talk to someone more privately during or after the workshop. I am going to check in with every one who leaves, and its fine to just walk by me, but you can also utilize me if you want to.

(Pass out sexual assault/domestic violence resource list.)

AGREEMENTS:
- We have a diversity of genders, bodies, sexualities, and experiences in the room - we'll try to make this discussion as inclusive and participatory as possible and we'll *try* to use gender neutral pronouns for participants and partners. Also, we use the word sex loosely in this discussion to encompass all sorts of getting it on (talking "dirty", smooching, making out, doing it, etc.)
- Survivors of sexual assault in the room, and that this presentation could possibly be triggering for some folks - we have a support person and we'll be aware of ourselves and others emotional states
- Most all of us have received conditioning thru this culture, ranging from body issues to imposed beauty standards to sexism and misogyny to heterosexism to religious/sexual morality, etc so it can be really hard to speak openly about sex. Let's not judge each others consensual sexual behaviors or interests in this space. (We'll try to make it easier to talk by having large & small group discussions and open ended questions)
- If you usually speak a lot, step back to give space to others. If you usually don't speak much, step up and give it a try.
- Don't name names or identifiable info during the workshop or afterward (please talk about the workshop later though...)
- Speak from your own experience
- Please address what's said, not the person saying it.

We know this can be tuff subject to approach openly and honestly especially among strangers. So we're gonna open up to you and be a little silly and ridiculous and we hope you'll open up to us.

This is where we do the puppet show. Email Down There if you want the script.
- Think about the factors, dynamics and issues that play into the way the characters give and receive consent; positive / negative examples of consent; some of the unspoken issues at play; some factors that can get in the way of real, honest consent; etc...

II. LARGE GROUP DISCUSSION (ABOUT 30 MIN)
Factors that play into the ways we give / receive and understand consent

PUPPET SHOW – Discuss issues we asked people to think about above.

RECOGNIZING BOUNDARIES – YOUR OWN AND OTHERS

- How do you give yourself or someone else space to figure out what you/ they want?
- Do you know what you want? How do figure this out for yourself?
- How do you communicate what you want or don't want?
- Have you ever been unsure? What did you do?
- How do you give a partner space to communicate what they want

- How do you know when someone else is consenting?
    - How do you know when someone wants to be kissed or to kiss you?
    - How are you sure they are fully present?
    - That they are excited to be doing what they are doing?
    - Do you account for cultural differences?

- How do people communicate their boundaries?
    - Have you interpreted passivity or silence as consent? What factors were at play?
    - Do you feel it's the other person's responsibility to say something if they aren't into what you're doing?
        - How often do you check in as things progress?
        - What signs do you look for? Verbal? Other signs?
        - When do you feel it's ok to use non-verbal signs? When isn't it?
        - o Note: It is commonly interpreted that silence=consent and verbal signs=non-consent.
        - Are the signals you are sending clear? Do your words match your body language? (ex. saying no while continuing movement); consistency in words and actions? How do you address it when someone else's words and body language don't match up? (ex. saying yes but moving away or not responding)
        - How do you react when someone expresses non-consent?
    - Consent in long-term relationships vs. hook up?
        - o What assumptions do you make once someone's consented?
        - o Have you made assumptions about consent with a long-term partner?
        - o How do different types of relationships impact how and when we talk about consent? (ahead of time / in the moment)

- How can you communicate about STI's (Sexually Transmitted Infections)?
    - o When might be a good time to bring this up?
    - o What is safe(r) sex to you?
    - o How can you help partners feel comfortable talking about this / bringing it up with you?
    - o How does how you feel about someone, your assumptions about them, or the type of relationship affect how you talk about STIs?

POWER AND PRIVILEGE
- What power dynamics might factor into communication and consent? (privilege, gender, sexual preferences, size, race, age, class, organizational structure, sexual histories)
- How do you address different histories or unequal power dynamics?
- How do you honor the experience of the person you're with when it has been different than yours?

- How do you bring differences up and communicate about them?
- How can we talk about histories of sexual assault?
- How can we bring it up? When?
- What about coming from a background where sexual assault is often the norm?
- How does inebriation effect consent giving / asking?
- How do you react when someone else expresses non-consent?
- In your social circle can someone expressing non-consent be seen as un-cool or un-liberated?
- How do sexuality and gender expression relate to consent, assumptions or perceptions?

SMALL GROUPS - PRACTICAL "TOOLS" (15 MIN)

Remind people to introduce themselves when they first get in groups. Clarify – we want groups to come back with ideas and specific examples to share so that everyone can take home knowledge, phrases, etc. Role play in groups if time/comfortable. Have each group start with a different group of questions and move on to the next group if they finish.

Giving and recognizing consent / non-consent
1.   What are ways to give consent? How do you (personally) expressed consent? What signs (verbal and non-verbal) do you look for to know if someone is consenting?
2.   What are ways to express non-consent? How have you (personally) expressed non-consent? What are signs (both verbal and non-verbal) that you look for to know someone is not consenting?

How to talk about consent with a partner
- When do you bring it up?
- How is this different for a long-term partner vs. a casual encounter?
- Ideas for improving communication around consent?
- What can you do if you or your partner aren't sure what you want in the moment?

Making consent hott
- What's hott about consent?
- How can we incorporate clear consent into "doin' it" and make it fun and erotic? (examples: practice verbal consent with massages; role play)

Communicating about STI's.
- How can you bring up STIs and your feelings about safe sex?
- When can you bring this up?
- What is safe(r) sex to you?
- How can you help partners feel comfortable talking about it / bringing it up with you?
- How does how you feel about someone, your assumptions about them, or the type of relationship affect how you talk about STIs?

VI. (RE)DEFINING CONSENT AND CLOSING (20 MIN)

REPORT BACK

DEFINITION OF CONSENT
- What are some key thoughts/ phrases / words for a "holistic" "Yes! Yes! Yes!" (which implicitly includes No).
- What are some key elements that need to be taken into account in a radical definition of consent?
- How do power and privilege relate to our ability to give, receive, and understand consent? How did the issues in that part of the discussion figure into your definition of consent?
- Did your definition change throughout the workshop?

WRAP UP
- Hope we opened up questions for people.
- This is an ongoing process in understanding our desires and boundaries and communicating this with others.
- Encourage you to talk about this in your communities, to break down barriers to talking openly about consent. Improving communication and understanding is both healthy for our relationships and can prevent problems.

myspace.com/downtherehealth

THE BASICS by Philly Stands Up

There are lots of folks who aren't familiar with the deliberate practice of getting consent. Some people know about it, but assume it applies only to people who've assaulted someone.
And many folks who talk about consent publicly still think to ourselves, "Shit, I probably should check in about consent every time I get busy, but it's not fun or sexy; it sounds like a big old drag!"

Learning the vocabulary of consent is like learning a foreign language. At first, you can spend a lot of time groping for words and awkwardly putting sentences together. These are the basics! Persistent practice will give you confidence to be creative, and you will eventually become fluent & able to express yourself in a way that feels less forced.

Discussions about consent echo similar ones folks were having at the beginning of the AIDS crisis--the initial resistance to using condoms gave way as it became clear safer sex could keep people alive. Today, condoms, gloves, dental dams and safer sex are a normal part of people's sexual lives and our shared dialogue about sex. Consent is a huge piece of healthy, affirming and safe sexuality, and we want to see consent check-ins become as normal as rubber and latex in public discourse and private practice.

When it comes to the actual mechanics of talking about consent, there are no set answers. Writing this article, we were continually struck by the ongoing nature of the work. It's a process, and it can be a struggle. We're peeling back layers of silence and shame about sex--it can seem terrifying. We're inspired to keep moving because we're excited for a world without sexual assault, where all sex is consensual, and people communicate their boundaries honestly in all of their relationships.

Philly Stands Up works with perpetrators of sexual assault. Our definition of assault is very broad--we roughly define assault as a situation where people's boundaries are violated, and there is a huge spectrum of actions that fit into our definition. Everyone needs to work on developing their consent vocabulary, but for perpetrators, it is especially important, since a perpetrator has failed to get consent in the past.

It is appropriate & necessary in the aftermath of sexual assault for a perpetrator to go to Consent 101. We made up that term to describe the learning process we talked about at the beginning of the article--in Consent 101 you are exploring the fundamental ideas and language of consent and communication; the basics, the main ideas, how it feels to practice consent and develop your consent vocabulary. This process can look really   different in different circumstances, but we want to emphasize that,

as a perpetrator, you can not deal with sexual assault without improving your communication skills. If you can't communicate your boundaries, ask about someone else's boundaries, and act appropriately once you know a person's boundaries, you shouldn't be in romantic relationships. We also want to emphasize that good communication and consent do NOT only apply to folks you have romantic and sexual relationships with. Trust and boundaries are key elements of any sort of relationship, whether it's based on friendship, organizing, work, kinship and/or romance. You have abundant opportunities to practice!

The most basic things to know & remember about consent are:
1) YOU ARE NEVER ENTITLED. You aren't entitled to sex or people's bodies or minds. You aren't entitled to sex because someone gave their consent last time, or it seems like they want it. It's your job to make sure that you & your partner's boundaries are on the table and respected, every time.

2) You DO deserve positive, fulfilling sexual experiences. The shame and stigma around assault can be overwhelming. People are greater than any of their individual actions--you are not solely defined by it, but you are accountable for it.

This can't be said without repeating: YOU ARE ARE NEVER ENTITLED

When you are tearing apart the negative patterns and poor communication that lead up to an assault, it can be overwhelming to imagine what getting consent actually entails. This is especially true in the heat of the moment, when you are face to face with a person you're interested in having romantic or sexual contact with. You should carefully and SPECIFICALLY think out your plan to talk about consent BEFORE you're in the sack with someone. If you do, you will be more likely to communicate clearly and less apt to cling to silence and shame. You should also make consent of all types a part of your relationships with all sorts of people--it's important to have consensual honest relationships across the board, and to be intentional as you create them.

We know that it's impossible to enter every situation knowing exactly what you want or what to expect--unpredictability is a part of what's exciting about any kind of relationship. The more you can be intentional about what you want out of a relationship or encounter, however, the easier it will be to navigate it with integrity. We've heard lots of perpetrators say, in the aftermath of an assault, "I didn't mean for things to happen the way they did." It's likely that a lot of people, after they've made mistakes, certainly regret it and would do it differently if they could. Knowing what acting with intention feels like is a key piece of healthy relationships for everybody, and maybe especially people with a history of sexual assault.

Another piece of the consent puzzle specific to perpetrators is disclosure. If someone does not have all the relevant information, they cannot give informed consent. Negotiating sexual contact in the present DOES include an assault in your past. This is really difficult to talk about, and also completely necessary. Once again, if you don't feel like you can negotiate that conversation, you should rethink your decision to be in a given romantic or sexual encounter. It's pretty simple: NOT disclosing BEFORE hooking up means you aren't engaging in full consent.

We must take a moment here to offer the following disclaimer: disclosure must fit in with the needs of the survivor first. Sexual assault for a survivor equals a loss of control. A survivor loses the ability to determine what happens to their body & surroundings. A huge part of the process of healing is regaining that lost sense of control. A perpetrator's accountability process must serve that imperative--if you disclose details about the assault that the survivor doesn't want communicated, you are repeating the violation.

There are ways to talk about consent and sexual assault without naming names or breaking boundaries, and we'll offer some suggestions below.

It is up to you to figure out what kind of disclosure is within a survivor's boundaries. If you don't know, you could explicitly ask them (if that would be appropriate), or see if you can find out through your collective support networks. If you don't know and can't find out, err on the side of caution. You can talk about having a history of breaking boundaries, and offer people the opportunity to ask more questions about what that looked like, without divulging sensitive details like names. Make sure you warn people in advance if you talk about details that might be triggering--you might be speaking to another survivor!

Talking about your history with perpetrating sexual assault is important for many reasons. Being accountable to your actions and your community means owning your mistakes and working hard to restore trust. This trust goes beyond partners or potential dates. It exists among friends, housemates, comrades, and folks with whom you do organizing work and activism.

We are doing this work because it's worth it; because we believe that radical change is not just possible, but necessary. Because we are struggling with oppression and injustice everyday and because that change and that possibility begins with ourselves; with our own relationships to each other. Because without genuine love, compassion and trust, we are all screwed.

Now onto the details! A great way to prepare to talk about consent is by role playing. Having a few handy ways to open conversation is both empowering and an effective way to make sure consent conversations happen. We offer a few specific scenarios below--practice these conversations alone, with a trusted friend, or even in a group of other folks who all want to become better communicators at a consent party. Think about them, write them down, speak them aloud.

Disclosure is hard. Let's be up front about that. It's hard for a lot of reasons:

1) We may feel shame. Ashamed of the actions we made, ashamed of how we hurt someone, ashamed that we didn't know what we were doing. Ashamed that we did know what we were doing.

2) Sex negativity is pervasive! Often, talking about an incident of sexual assault means we have to skate near or on top of the icy issue of S-E-X. Yikes! Even in cultures and communities where dishing about sex is accepted or encouraged, most of us have been exposed to negative messages about sex for most of our lives! This can make us feel disgraced, dirty, humiliated, and exposed, and not in the good way...

3) Fear of losing friends/dates. It is a very real possibility that once you talk to some folks about your past, they will feel nervous, angry, scared, or confused. Fear of losing friends or potential dates is totally valid fear.

4) Killing the vibe. It might be hard to imagine a steamy moment with a new friend or date. Where the music is perfect, the sound of the passing trains is so picturesque, y'all are getting each others' humor, your hands naturally fall into just the right top/bottom position, it's awesome! How do you bust that vibe with something as heavy as your sexual assault past? Well, like we said earlier, folks used to (and lots still do...) say the same thing about condoms. But there are infinite ways to be creative and smooth while remaining honest and for real. And hey, what's a bigger turn on than bangin' communication skills? No seriously, nothing.

one more thing: These conversations can go a million different ways. It's important to remember that you can't control the reaction and feelings of the person/people you are talking to. Focus on your own goals for this conversation. Your goals might include: staying honest, not omitting certain information, just getting through what you want to say, speaking calmly, etc. However, you should be ready for reactions. The person/people you tell might feel upset, mad, supportive, sad. They might not want to talk about it. Additionally, this might be much bigger than one conversation over tea. However this goes, it is important that you allow them to have that reaction. Take a deep breath and just be brave...

Ok, let's go through three potential scenarios of disclosure. The first, is disclosing to a friend or people that you know well in a non romantic way. The second, is disclosing to a new friend; someone you don't know very well who you don't have a romantic relationship with. The third is how to talk to someone about your past right before you might cuddle/make-out/ have sex/ play/ do-it with.

1. YOU KNOW THEM WELL

why it's important:
- so they hear it from you before they hear it somewhere else.
- this is a crucial way to be accountable to your community.
- you are doing important, hard work of disclosure. You are deepening your trust. And hey, after you make the first move in your vulnerability, maybe they will feel brave enough to share something with you…
- your own healing. Keeping a big scary secret can eat away at you.

your pal/housemate: here's the scenario…

It's a lazy sunday morning. You are both awake, sipping tea while you cook a leisurely breakfast. The conversation moves into talking about dates and sex. Now might be the time… Starting the conversation might be the hardest part. Here are some ideas for how to start:

+ "I've been wanting to talk to you about something that's going on with me…"
+ "Listen, I want you to hear this from me…"
+ "I'm working hard to be accountable to my community, people I care about. I care about you. Part of that is talking openly and honestly about behavior I've asserted in the past…"

1415

2. YOU DON'T KNOW THEM WELL

why it's important:
* while it may feel riskier to disclose to someone that you don't have established trust with, or it may feel irrelevant because they aren't in your immediate friend group it is important to disclose anyway…*
-you do not want to repeat the experience of violating boundaries by with holding information.
-a radical goal we have is to break the cycle of assault. It starts here…

a new friend/ potential organizing buddy. here's the scenario:

Your hanging out at the park eating plums. Your hands and faces are kind of sticky, but you're still having a good conversation. They are a new buddy, but someone you are obviously going to be spending time with. There's a lull...

ways to start...

+ "I know we just met, but I really want to talk to you about this..."
+ "So, I make it a real priority for myself to be upfront with people I meet..."
+ "I'm really excited to be friends/organizing buddies with you, so I want to start right."

then maybe,
"In the past, I've violated/crossed boundaries. Talking to people about it is part of my process/ way of staying accountable. If you want to talk more about it, I'm open." (then of course, follow up and be available to talk with them if you say you will).

3. POTENTIAL HOOK UP

why it's important:
- it is NOT consensual if they don't know all the information they might need to make an informed decision.
- you are establishing trust.
- you are setting the scene for all kinds of other important communication that should take place around sex (sharing pertinent health information, using barriers, checking in about boundaries, checking in about gender/body identity, etc.)

a potential date or hook up is upon yall. here's the scenario:

The two of you have been around the same scene for a while, but really hit it off at a puppet workshop. You were both flirting with each other via your puppets. It was totally hot and adorable. Now you're back at their house after drinking tea. There have been some deliberate hand squeezes, arm brushes, and lots of flirty talk. You kiss...

here are some ways to start…

+"I'm into you/ I want to do XYZ with you/ this feels good. But before we go any further, I want to check in about a couple things…"

- "In the past I've broken peoples' boundaries, and I'm really committed to talking about that and making sure it never happens again…"

- "I think consent is hot and important. I want you to know that I'm working on respecting peoples' boundaries and bodies and I have a history of struggling with that. I'm open to talking about that now or some other time, but I want you to know that."

- "I want you to know that I wouldn't be here if I didn't trust myself to seek out and respect your boundaries…" (If you can't honestly and confidently say this, you should NOT be intimate with

If you can get through any of these scenarios, regardless of how they go, you should pat yourself on the back, give yourself a hug and treat

your self to something sweet, because you just took a really big step and exercised a LOT of bravery.

All of these scenarios are vague starters to doing really hard work. But, if you are committed to change and radical revisioning of how we interact with one another, you've got to be committed to consent. The culture of consent is one which we are all responsible for shaping. Commitment to consent does not mean being the make-out police, being a stick in the mud, being overly sensitive, or any other hoo-ha type of myth that you might think of. The moment of an assault and the painful aftermath has a ripple effect through the community and reveals how interconnected we all are to each other; tangled up in matrices of relation to one another. While we often see how harm to one or a few touches so many of us, the reverse is trues as well. Positive, trusting, respectful, creative relationships and friendships are part of our survival. This tangible type of love is what moves us closer and closer to collective liberation. Our liberation, autonomy, and progress are bound up in eachother. We need every member of our big beautiful community to flex those muscles of compassion, thoughtfulness and integrity. Once you practice and learn yourself within the context of consent, you may be able to tap into creativity, confidence and communication you never thought possible. And we don't know what's hotter than that…

Signs to look for in a battering personality

Below is a list of signs that are seen in people who beat their partners or spouses. Even just one of the following can be a form of domestic violence or abuse. The last four signs are almost always seen only if the person is a batterer —even one of the following incidents can be abuse. If a person has several of the behaviors (say 3 or more) there is a strong potential for physical violence —the more signs a person has, the more life threatening the situation could become. For simplicities sake the following is written in he(abuser)/she(victim) scenarios. This is not to imply that just men are abusers and just women are victims. Domestic violence is manifested in many forms and within many sorts of relationships, it is not confined to gender roles

1. **Jealousy:** After the beginning of a relationship, an abuser will always say that his jealousy is a sign of love; jealousy has nothing to do with love. It is a sign of insecurity and possessiveness. He will question his partner about who she talks to, accuse her of flirting, or be jealous of time she spends with family, friends or children. As the jealousy progresses, he may call her frequently during the day or drop by unexpectedly. He may refuse to let her work for fear she'll meet someone else, or even do strange behaviors such as checking her car mileage or asking friends to watch her.

2. **Controlling Behavior:** At first the batterer will say that this behavior is because he's concerned for his partner's safety, her need to use her time well, or her need to make decisions. He will be angry if his partner is "late" coming back from the store or an appointment, he will question her closely about where she went, who she talked to. As this behavior gets worse, he may not let his partner make any personal decisions about the house, her clothing, going to church; he may keep all of the money or even make her ask permission to leave the house or room.

3. **Quick Involvement:** Many battered women dated or knew their abuser less than 6 months before they were engaged or living together. He comes on like a whirl-wind "you're the only person I will ever talk to," or "I've never felt loved like this by anyone." He needs someone desperately, and will pressure his partner to commit to him.

4. **Unrealistic Expectations:** He is very dependent on his partner for all of his needs; he expects her to be the perfect spouse, parent, lover, friend. He will say things like, "If you love me, I'm all you need —you're all I need." She is supposed to take care of everything for him emotionally and in the home.

5. **Isolation:** The abuser tries to cut his partner off from all resources. Is she has men friends, she is a "whore," if she has women friends, she is a lesbian, if she is close to her family, "she is tied to the apron strings." He accuses people who are her supporters of "causing trouble," he may want to live in the country without a phone, he may not let her use the car, or he may try to keep her from working or going to school.

6. **Blames Others for his Problems:** If he is chronically unemployed, someone is always doing him wrong, out to get him. He may make mistakes and then blame them on his partner for upsetting him and keeping him from concentrating on doing his job. He will tell his partner she is at fault for almost anything that goes wrong.

7. **Blames Others for his Feelings:** He will tell his partner "you make me mad," or "you're hurting me by not doing what I ask," or "I can't help being angry." He really makes the decisions about what he thinks and feels, but will use his feelings to manipulate his partner. Harder to catch are his claims that "you make me happy," or "you control how I feel."

8. **Hypersensitivity:** The abuser is easily insulted, he claims his feelings are "hurt" when he's really very mad, or he takes the slightest set backs as personal attacks. He will "rant and rave" about the injustice of things that have happened to him –things that are really just part of living like being asked to work overtime, getting a traffic ticket, being told that something he does is annoying, being asked to help with chores.

9. **Cruelty to Animals or Children:** This is a person who punishes animals brutally or is insensitive to their pain or suffering; he may expect children to be capable of doing things far beyond their ability (whips a two year old for wetting his diaper) or he may tease children or young brothers siblings until they cry. (60% of abusers who beat the partner they are with also beat their children). He may not allow children to eat at the table or expect them to keep to their room all evening while he is home.

10. **"Playful" Use of Force in Sex:** This abuser may like to throw his partner down and hold her during sex, we may want to act out fantasies during sex where his partner is helpless (and not consenting). He's letting his partner know that the idea of 'rape' excites him. He may show little concern about whether his partner wants to have sex and use sulking or anger to manipulate her into compliance. He may start having sex with his partner while she is sleeping, or demand sex while she is ill or tired.

11. **Verbal Abuse:** In addition to saying things that are meant to be cruel and hurtful, this can be seen by the man degrading his partner, crushing her, running down any of her accomplishments. The man will tell her that she's stupid and unable to function without him. This may involve waking her up to verbally abuse her or not letting her sleep.

12. **Rigid Sex Roles:** The abuser expects his partner to serve him; will say she must stay at home, that she must obey him in all things –even things that are criminal in nature. The abuser will see women/people of color/ bisexuals/ the physically impaired/ the young/ old as inferior to men/ Caucasian/ straight/ gay/ abled, more stupid, unable to be a whole person without a relationship.

13. **Dr.Jeckell &Mr.Hyde:** Many partner's are confused by their abuser's "sudden" changes in mood –they will describe that one minute he's nice and the next minute he explodes or that he's 'crazy.' Explosiveness and mood swings are typical of people who beat their partners; these behaviors can be related to other characteristics, such as hypersensitivity.

14. **Past Battering:** The abuser may say he has hit partners in the past, but that they made him do it. His partner may hear from relatives or ex-spouses that the person is abusive. A batterer may beat any partner he is with; situational circumstances do not make a person an abusive personality.

15. **Threats of Violence:** This would include any threat of physical force meant to control his partner. Most people do not threaten their partners, but a batterer will try to excuse his behavior by saying, "everybody talks like that."

16. **Breaking or Striking Objects:** This behavior is used as a punishment (breaking loved possessions), but is mostly used to terrorize his partner into submission. The abuser may beat on tables with his fists or throw objects near his partner. Again, this is a very remarkable behavior, only very immature people beat on objects in the presence of other people in order to threaten them.

17. **Any Force During an Argument:** This may involve an abuser holding his partner down, physically restraining her from leaving the room, any pushing or shoving. (The abuser may hold his partner against a wall and say "you are going to listen to me.")

Safe Sex is More Than Just Latex

<u>If you answer yes to any of the following questions, you may be experiencing abuse:</u>
Do you feel pushed to have sex when you don't want to?
Do you ever have sex to "keep the peace"?
Does your partner want sex after a fight when you don't want it?
Have you ever just laid there during sex because resisting felt more risky?
Has your partner ever started sex with you while you were sleeping?
Has your partner refused to practice safe sex when you asked her to?
Have you ever felt that your partner used sex to control or punish you?
Has she ever given you a hard time about wanting to stop midway through?
Has your partner forced you to have sex against your will?
Does your partner withhold sex or affection, or does she demand it on her terms?
Does your partner use sexual name-calling against you?
Does your partner ever put you down or make fun of you about sex?
Have you ever had sex with her because you were tired of resisting?
Does your partner accuse you of having affairs?
Does your partner threaten to have, or have affairs when you both have agreed to be monogamous?
Does she put you down during sex?
Does your partner talk with others (ex-partner, friends, etc.) about your sexual inadequacies?
Does your partner demand that you tell her your fantasies?
Does your partner make you feel ashamed about your sexual desires or fantasies?
Has your partner violated your limits, boundaries, or safe words?
In the context of S/M, are you ever confused about when scenes begin and end?

A Personal Bill of Rights

I have the right:

To ask for a date without being crushed if the answer is "no"
To refuse a date without feeling guilty
To suggest activities
To refuse any activities, even if my date is excited about them
To have my own feelings
To choose to go to parties alone without feeling like I have to pair up with someone
To say I think a friend's information is wrong or her/his actions unfair
To tell someone I don't like her/him to interrupt me
To have my limits respected
To spend my money they way I want to, even if it's foolish
To tell my partner I want affection
To tell my partner I want physical closeness
To refuse sex with anyone who just took me out on an expensive date
To start a relationship slowly, to say, "I want to get to know you better before I get involved."
To be myself without changing to suit others
To tell my partner I want sex
To refuse sex, or any other intimacy, anytime
To be told a relationship is changing and not blame myself, or change myself to keep it going
To an equal relationship with a man or a woman
To not be dominate or be dominated
To be quiet or assertive and not be misunderstood
To act one way with one person and a different way with someone else

JOE BIEL INTERVIEWS CINDY CRABB

(originally published in *Maximum Rocknroll*, 2006)

JOE BIEL: I've always appreciated the articles in *Doris* about history and it seems that over time *Doris* has evolved continually. What determines the content of an issue?

CINDY CRABB: I think our society is deeply dependent on our ignorance. They want us to believe that we are isolated and we don't have the power to make fundamental changes in our world, but when you study history, especially revolutionary history and the history of movements for social change, you see that we really do have power, and that change is happening, despite all the nightmarish-ness of the world we live in. History has definitely helped keep me sane. But, basically, I usually try and have at least a tiny bit of history or historical perspective in each issue. I want *Doris* to evoke a whole range of emotion and thinking: some laughter, some critical thinking and figuring things out, some opening of secrets and silences.

BIEL: Can you talk about your family's relationship with your writing?

CRABB: There was definitely some awkward years where I wanted my dad and mom and grandparents to know that I was doing something with my life, and I tried to explain about my zine, and even made a couple edited copies to give them. Since I could never talk openly about it or really show them what I was doing, I just had to accept that they thought I wasn't doing anything with my life. Eventually my relationship with my dad got a lot better, and he's always really happy and supportive about what I'm doing. I told my grandparents about the book and told them it wasn't family appropriate. They're sort of hurt, but they're also 90 years old and I think they understand how much times have changed and that they probably wouldn't really want to read it. I just laugh about it and tell them they can read the next one. One of my aunts read it, and when I sent it to her I thought she would never talk to me again, but she called me after she read it and she was just going on and on about how great it was and how sorry she was that I had to go through all that alone.

BIEL: What prompted such a heavy discussion of assault and rape?

CRABB: When I first started reading zines, there was a lot of writing about assault and rape. There was a lot of valid and powerful anger and I just don't find writing like that anymore, which is sad because there is still so much work that needs to be done. People are still getting raped and not even knowing to call it rape. People are still assaulting their friends and not being able to own up to what they've done. So I did want to remind people that this is a very real issue that hasn't gone away. I had always planned to write about girl gangs when I got to the letter G. It just happened that when I got there I was dealing pretty heavily with my own abuse history stuff, especially about how no one I'd been in a serious relationship which had ever been able to be actively supportive. I didn't think that the sexual issues I had that stemmed from abuse were unusual or that they should have been particularly hard for my partners to see or deal with. It made me really depressed that I couldn't get the support I needed. I hoped that by putting the call out for contributions to a zine about supporting survivors, that I could help start to open up a place for people to learn from each other about abuse, the effects of abuse, and how to be supportive. I was sick of how survivors had to carry all the burden of healing ourselves and educating our partners. I was exhausted and desperate and trying to pass the work on. I didn't realize what I was getting myself into.

BIEL: As a musician, artist, and writer, do you feel that these components feed into each other creatively, or just as far as people being familiar with the many facets of what you do and your work?

CRABB: Am I an artist and musician? That is so sweet of you to say! Seriously! I don't really think of myself as either of those things. I pretty much have to write. I don't think I have to draw and play music, but I do need some kind of release. The drawings help me step back from the more complicated writing. They help me use a more forgiving part of my brain. I get to laugh and it helps me go on. Also, they help me remember to get to the heart of things, so I suppose the writing and drawing do feed each other. They're also sort of a crutch. When I need to make a transition in one of the stories, I can just put a drawing in and it helps get your brain ready for something else and I don't have to work so hard on figuring out a good way to make the transition literarily. As far as music goes, I mostly do it because there still aren't enough girls in bands. There aren't enough girls screaming.

BIEL: Do you think about your influence or how people will respond to your ideas?

CRABB: I wouldn't wish my life on anyone. It's a weird defense mechanism about the zine. I don't think anyone reads it and a lot of times I don't even think I wrote it. I am a really closed in and private person, and I have a really hard time letting people close to me or telling them things that are important to me, so I guess if I really thought people read my zine I don't know if I could write it the way I do. I'm trying to normalize things rather than influence. Like, we all know that TV rots us, that beauty standards are really destructive, that feeling is important, that being challenged to think deeply is actually really great, and that there's a whole other kind of world we could be living, a world based on being nice to each other and trying to understand each other and sharing and celebrating and working and seeing usefulness in our work, and all that kind of stuff. I really believe most people know this world is what they would want, even if it is just a vision they think of as childish that they have buried deep within themselves and it's surrounded by scar tissue and cynicism.

BIEL: Zines often have a reputation for being selective windows into people's lives but your zines feel extraordinarily honest.

CRABB: *Doris* is mostly about what goes on deeper inside my head and heart. It is not at all truly reflective of my whole self. I spend a lot of time being irritated and confused. I am honest in my writing, but not all the stories are completely true stories. Most of them are, but a few of them are fictionalized to protect people, or to protect myself, or because it just works nicely literarily. Like we didn't really use our shoelaces to try and tie the rain tarp on to the tent, but it felt like that's what we did.

BIEL: You drop numerous references to anarchism and feminism in your writing through value choices and anecdotes so casually.
CRABB: I drop references to anarchism and feminism because they are at the core of my belief system, and they inform pretty much everything I do. I think it is helpful for people to see these beliefs in a context of someone's daily life, because so often they're just seen as abstractions. I also want to help encourage people to look at the belief systems they hold and the reasons for their actions. That's what makes humans amazing. We can look at our actions and our thought processes and how we relate to other people, and look at why we're doing the things we do, and we can challenge ourselves and change, becoming better people. My mom was raised Christian Scientist, and believed that all people are fundamentally good, and she really passed that on to me. I went to an alternative school and we set our own study plans, and learned from each other not just from the teachers. I hung around smart people who were trying to change the world in concrete ways, and I tried to learn to think deeply and for myself. In the beginning there were a lot of quick developments—like squatting was going to bring about the revolution, or music was going to, or we better learn to be self-sustaining and stop being part of consumer society. Quickly though, I could see that there was no one thing, no one way of thinking that was perfect and right. I spent a lot of time trying to value women and get rid of the sexist parts of me that looked to men for approval and answers. Even if there is no revolution, even if we don't create an anarchist world, anything we can do is better than nothing, since it has been proven over and over in history that power corrupts.

BIEL: In my experience, many people, punks included, have quick rebuttals to anarchism and feminism—they essentially write it off as useless theory, impractical, or idealistic.
CRABB: I never saw punk as being essentially political. I see it coming from a place that is a big fuck you to all convention, and that embraces anger and says we're going to make our outsides look like our insides and our insides feel like shit, because this world is shit and here we are. Deal with it. If I have to argue about this, I would probably talk about my mom's life and the choices she had—get married and have kids—and then how much has changed because of the feminist movement—birth control, battered women's shelters, and the radical idea that women have the right to be safe in their homes, the fact that there's women getting published now and included in required reading in schools. I think people have such an ignorance of history; it's sad and so disempowering. I would try and spend more time talking nicely with people who haven't been exposed to anarchist or feminist ideas, and who are open to talking and thinking and figuring out what they think, and less time on people who want to shoot you down. That's my advice.

thanks

to all The amazing people who helped make This happen!

resources

BOOKS

SURVIVORS GUIDE TO SEX by STACI HAINES

INVISIBLE GIRLS - PATTI FEUEREISEN   COURAGE TO HEAL by Bass + DAVIS · ALLIES IN HEALING by DAVIS

MEN'S WORK - PAUL KIVEL

HOLY VIRILITY: the SOCIAL CONSTRUCTION of MASCULINITY - REYNAUD

REDEFINING OUR RELATIONSHIPS - WENDY OMATIC   THE ETHICAL SLUT

THE WILL TO CHANGE: MEN, MASCULINITY + LOVE - bell hooks

MEN + INTIMACY - ABBOT   CRACKING THE ARMOR - KAUFMAN

WEBSITES

campus - adr. org/CMHER/ Report Resources / Editions 6-1/ stopping-rape. html · men stopping rape exercises + group activities   myspace.com/downtherehealth

generationfive.org   myspace. com/phillyspissedandstandsup

dorisdorisdoris.com/resources   incite-national.org

cARA-seattle.org   men can stoprape.org   icarusproject.net

xyonline.net   a calltomen.com   radicalsurvivorasheville.blogspot.com

girlarmy.org   notherapedocumentary.org

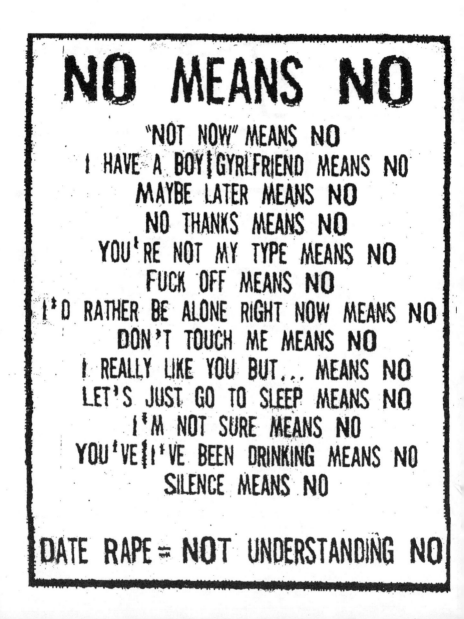